D0513293

EVEN MORE WAYS TO BE THE BEST AT EVERYTHING

Written by Steve Martin
Illustrated by Martin Remphry
Edited by Jen Wainwright
Designed by Zoe Quayle

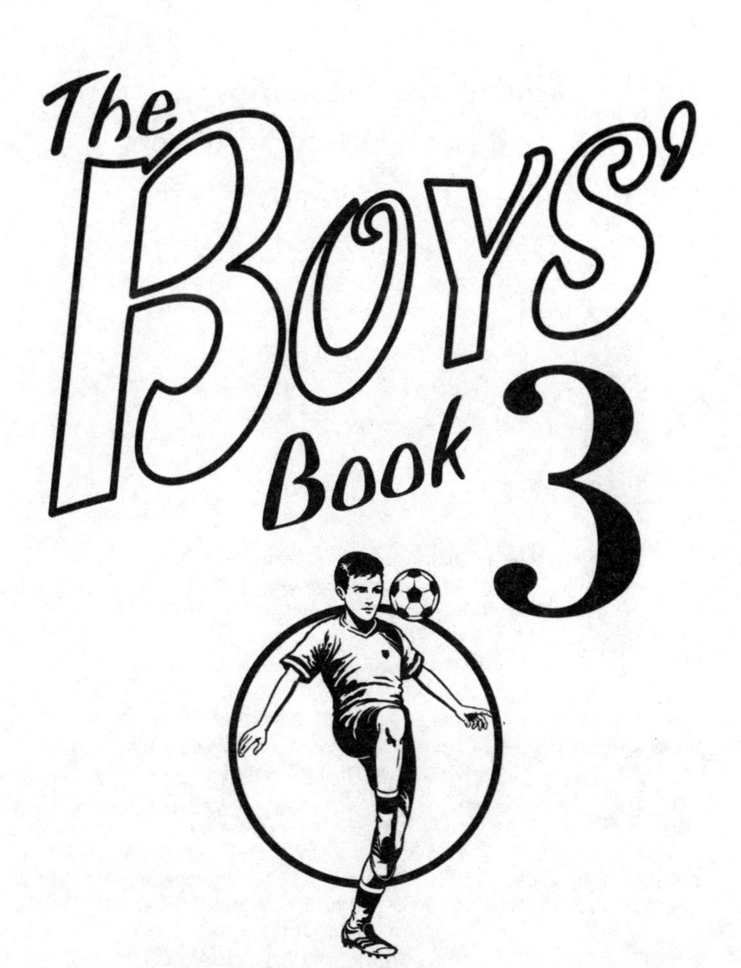

EVEN **MORE** WAYS TO BE THE BEST AT EVERYTHING

Buster Books

First published in Great Britain in 2009 by Buster Books,
an imprint of Michael O'Mara Books Limited,
9 Lion Yard, Tremadoc Road, London SW4 7NQ

www.mombooks.com/busterbooks

Cover design by Angie Allison (from an original design by www.blacksheep-uk.com)
Cover illustration by Paul Moran

A CIP catalogue record for this book is available from the British Library.

ISBN: 978-1-906082-75-8

2 4 6 8 10 9 7 5 3 1

Printed and bound in England by Clays Ltd, St Ives plc

Papers used by Buster Books are natural, recyclable products
made from wood grown in sustainable forests. The manufacturing processes
conform to the environmental regulations of the country of origin.

NOTE TO READERS

The publisher and author disclaim any liability for accidents or injuries that may occur as a result of the information given in this book.

To be the best at everything, you'll need to use your best common sense at all times, particularly when heat or sharp objects are involved.

Make sure you follow safety precautions and advice from responsible adults. Ask an adult's permission before you leave the house, especially if you're going near a river or a busy road. Always wear appropriate safety gear, stay within the law and local rules, and be considerate of other people.

CONTENTS

HOW TO BECOME AN EXPERT

Being the best is about impressing people, and a great way to convince everyone you are very, very clever, and extremely important, is to become an expert. The best way to become an expert is to become an '-ologist'.

You can easily get certain '-ologies' under your belt at school by studying subjects like biology or technology. However, if you don't like these, don't worry, as there's an -ology for just about everything. Here are a few ideas to get you started:

Palaeontology – Studying fossils.
Archaeology – Studying history by searching for, and digging up, old ruins and objects.
Egyptology – Studying Ancient Egypt.
Mythology – Studying myths.
Ecology – Studying the environment and the animals and plants that live in it.
Geology – Studying rocks.
Ornithology – Studying birds.

As you can see, -ologies sound pretty impressive. Why say you go bell-ringing when you can tell people that you're an expert 'campanologist'?

CHOOSING YOUR OWN -OLOGY

If you can't decide which -ology to go for, here are a few tips:

- The most impressive -ologies are those that are hard to pronounce, especially if people don't know what the word means. For instance, you could become an 'ichthyologist' (an expert in fish), or a 'vexillologist' (an expert in flags).

• Some -ologies are easier to become an expert in than others as you don't need qualifications. For example, 'cryptozoology' is the study of animals that may or may not exist. So, if you go off hunting for the Loch Ness Monster or a Yeti – even if you don't find one – you are a cryptozoologist.

You can, of course, invent your own -ologies to make your interests seem important. 'Eating-ice-cream-ology' won't impress anyone, but experts have a trick – they use the ancient Latin language to create -ologies. The Latin for 'to have dinner' is 'cenare' and the Latin for 'ice' is 'glacies', so an expert in eating ice cream for dinner could be a 'cenareglaciesologist'. Now there you have a tasty field of expertise that will make sure everyone is amazed by your intelligence.

HOW TO ANNOY PEOPLE IN A LIFT

You know you're a funny guy, right? Well, even top comedians need to practise their hilarious gags. A lift is the perfect place to brush up on your humour, as your audience can't go anywhere. Try out these tips and see how long their patience holds out.

- Salute and say, 'Welcome aboard!' every time someone gets into the lift.
- Sit down and start barking like a dog.

- Pretend to be a flight attendant. Tell people how to fasten their seatbelts, where the nearest exits are, and what happens if the lift lands on water.
- Ask everyone for a high-five at each floor.
- Suggest a game of charades, and start to act things out.
- Open your bag and, while looking inside, say, 'I'll get you some food as soon as I can.'
- Spin around and around in the centre of the lift.

HOW TO MAKE A BALLOON CHANGE COLOUR

What happens when you stick a pin into a balloon? There's a loud, 'Pop!' and you're left with the shreds of a burst balloon. Right? Not any more. Find out how to wow people by popping a balloon and have it magically change colour.

You Will Need:

• a red balloon • a blue balloon • sticky tape
• a pencil • a pin

WHAT YOU DO

1. Put a double-sided loop of sticky tape on the biggest part of your blue balloon.

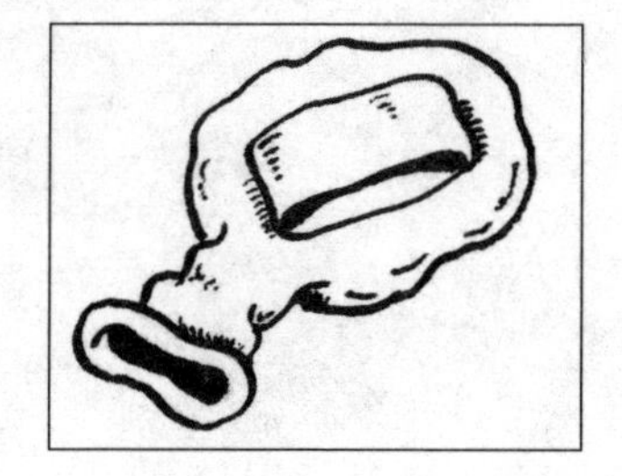

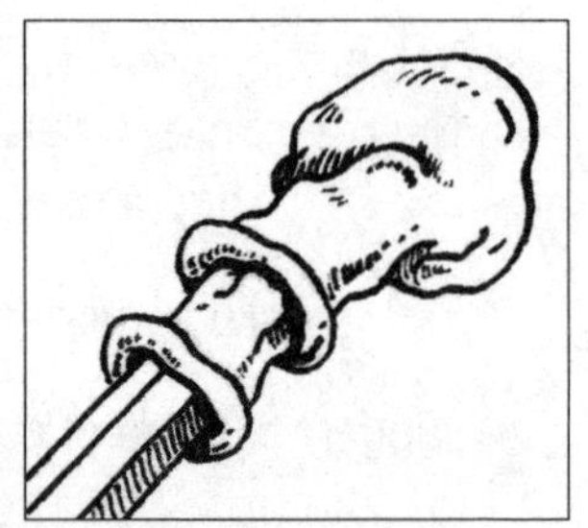

2. Slide a pencil into the neck of the blue balloon and use this to help you push it inside the red one. You may have to work the red balloon down the pencil bit by bit. When you've finished, remove the pencil carefully.

3. Blow up the blue balloon (this will blow up the red one as well), and tie a knot in the bottom.

4. Stand in front of your audience holding the balloons. All they will see is the red balloon on the outside.

5. Find where the sticky tape is, by looking through the red balloon, and then jab it with a pin at this point.

The red balloon will burst with a loud bang and you will be left holding the blue balloon. To anybody watching, it looks as if the red balloon has suddenly, magically changed colour.

HOW TO MOVE OBJECTS USING THE POWER OF YOUR MIND

Moving an object using mind power will not only amaze your friends, but it will astound you as well. This is because the technique you are about to learn is not a trick – you really will learn how to move an object by mind control.

All you need is a pendulum and a friend. A pendulum is just a weight at the bottom of a piece of string. Anything will do for the weight. For example, you could tie a set of house keys, or a lump of plasticine or sticky tack to one end of the string. Whatever object you choose, tie it so that there is about 30 cm of string between the weight and the other end of the string when you hold it.

Once you've made the pendulum, you are ready to begin.

WHAT YOU DO

1. Tell your friend to hold the top of the string between his thumb and index finger so the weight is hanging down and not moving.

2. Inform him that you are going to move the weight using only mind power.

3. To create an air of mystery, and make what you are going to do seem even more impressive, place your fingers on the sides of your head, rub your temples and squint with concentration.

4. Now, tell the weight to start moving in a circle. You need to keep repeating the instruction out loud:

'Move round in a circle ... round and round ... round and round ....' Keep saying this over and over again and the weight will begin to move in a circle.

5. After a while, give a new instruction. 'Now, start moving in the opposite direction ... round and round in the other direction ... round and round in the other direction ....' You and your friend will both watch in surprise as the weight slowly begins to move the other way, just as you ordered it to.

6. For your next instruction, tell the weight to move backwards and forwards. Again, speak the instruction aloud. 'Move backwards and forwards ... backwards and forwards ... backwards and forwards ....' You will soon see the weight obeying your command.

HOW IT WORKS

By now, you're probably half-amazed and half-terrified. Don't worry, though, there's nothing spooky about what is going on. What you've just learned is how effective the power of suggestion can be.

When you tell the weight to move in a certain direction, your friend's finger and thumb move the string so that the weight goes in the direction you command. The movement is so slight that your friend doesn't even know that he is doing it.

So, you really can move objects with the power of the mind. What your friend doesn't realize, however, is that it's his mind making the movement happen, not yours.

HOW TO TOSS A CABER

The caber toss is a famous and important part of the Highland Games in Scotland. A caber is the trunk of a pine tree, with one end thinner than the other. As you might imagine it is very, very heavy. Contestants in this event lift up the huge cabers and toss them into the air, so that they turn over in mid-air, and land on their fatter end before falling flat.

TRY IT YOURSELF

The winner of the caber toss is not the person who throws it the furthest – it's actually all about accuracy. In order to win, a contestant needs to get his caber to land in the twelve o'clock position from the place he threw it. Even boys who are the best at everything shouldn't attempt to toss a full-sized caber, but if you want to hold your own Highland Games, then a 'broom-handle toss' will work just as effectively. Get together with your friends and see who can get their 'caber' to land straightest. Here's a handy step-by-step guide to the best caber-tossing technique.

1. Take your broom handle (or a pole of a similar size) to a wide open space, and check that there are no members of the public who might be about to get whacked by a flying caber.

2. Bend down and lean the caber against your shoulder so that it is standing upright. Then lift it off the ground.

3. Move your hands to the bottom and clasp them, palm upwards, around the base of the caber.

4. Move the caber up to about elbow height, and keep the weight balanced against your shoulder. Now you are in the throwing position.

5. Take a short run-up, gaining momentum slowly. This is called the 'approach'.

6. Throw your caber upwards and forwards slightly by jerking your clasped hands sharply upwards.

7. The caber should follow a path as shown, landing other way up. Its end should hit the ground as it stands upright before falling flat.

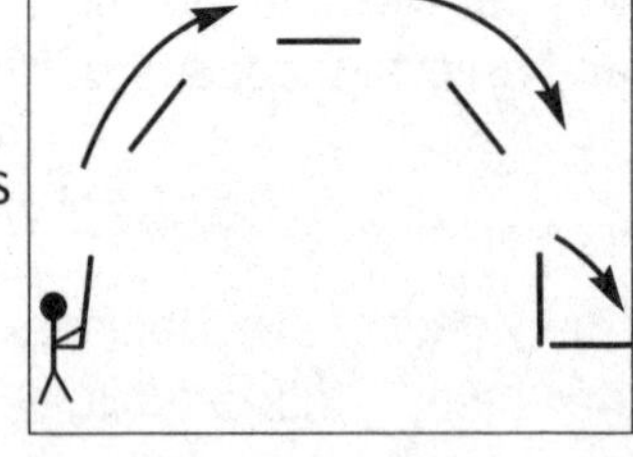

HOW TO BEAT A LIE-DETECTOR TEST

No good spy would ever give anything away. If you ever find yourself captured by enemy agents, you need to keep your secrets closely guarded.

However, lying to the enemy is tricky if they have lie-detector machines. If you are captured, you may be wired to one of these and it will show your enemies when you are lying. So, if you are going 'undercover', you need to know how to beat the machine.

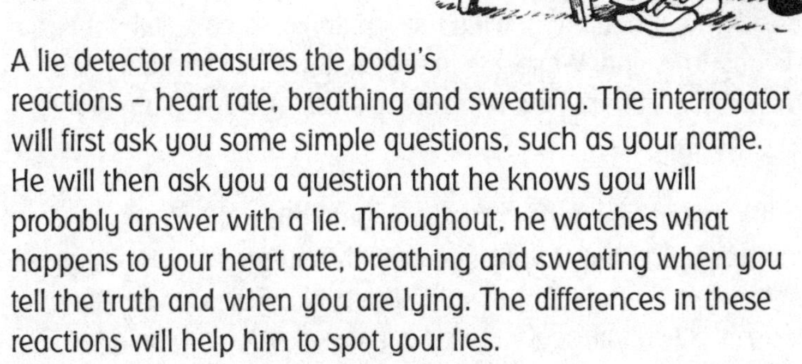

A lie detector measures the body's reactions – heart rate, breathing and sweating. The interrogator will first ask you some simple questions, such as your name. He will then ask you a question that he knows you will probably answer with a lie. Throughout, he watches what happens to your heart rate, breathing and sweating when you tell the truth and when you are lying. The differences in these reactions will help him to spot your lies.

Your job is to confuse the lie detector. The trick is to scare yourself. Think of whatever terrifies you the most – for instance rats, spiders, or heights – during all the questions. By increasing your stress level for all answers – true or false – you will confuse the machine so it cannot give an accurate reading.

HOW TO BE A RODEO STAR

Howdy, Partner! So, you want to ride the rodeo? Well, if you're very brave and a little bit crazy, then saddle up, Cowboy. You've got some broncos to ride.

The sport known today as 'rodeo' began in the 1800s, when cowboys working on ranches in America's Wild West would display their skills in rounding up herds of cattle for branding. Nowadays, rodeo is considered a highly competitive sport, with cowboys and cowgirls fighting to stay on their bucking and rearing horses to have a chance of winning big prize money.

RIDE 'EM COWBOY!

First, get yourself a horse or a bull. If you don't fancy the idea of riding a bull, stick to horses for now. It has to be a horse that isn't accustomed to being ridden. The horse is kept in a pen beside the rodeo ring (called the 'chute') to keep it still until you are ready to ride. While it is in the chute, check to make sure the saddle, stirrups and reins are fixed securely – you're going to need them.

Put your left foot in the left stirrup, grab the saddle with your left hand, and pull yourself up onto the horse, swinging your right leg over and into the right stirrup. Now, as if rodeo riding wasn't difficult enough, the rules only allow you to hold the reins with one hand.

The gate of the chute will open and you're off. As soon as you get on the horse, it will arch its back, leap into the air and try to throw you off.

All you have to do is to hold on. If you can stay on the horse for eight seconds, you've completed the ride. Try to ride with style, as you score points for how well you ride, and the person with the most points at the end is the winner. Holding one arm (the one that isn't busy hanging on to the reins) high in the air looks really cool.

Be careful not to touch the horse with your free hand, as this will get you disqualified from the competition.

Try and find a rhythm as the horse bucks and rears, and move your body with this rhythm to stay balanced. Shout, 'Yee-ha!' and 'Ride 'em, Cowboy!' as often as possible – you don't get any points for this, but it's fun.

Finally, if you've managed to stay on the bronco, a 'pick up rider' will ride up next to you and help you get off the horse.

If you are skilful enough to have scored the most points during your bucking bronco ride, then congratulations! You will be awarded some prize money and, instead of a trophy, you'll get a much sought-after engraved, silver rodeo belt buckle.

RODEO REPARTEE

It's also important to talk like a rodeo star. Here are a few terms to get you started:

Biting The Dust: Being thrown off the horse.

Bronco: A horse that isn't 'broken' – that isn't trained to have a rider on its back.

High Roller: A horse that jumps high when it tries to buck you off.

Tenderfoot: Someone who is new to the rodeo.

HOW TO TERRIFY YOUR FRIENDS

This quick and easy trick will leave even the most fearless of your friends quaking in his boots. Read on to find out how.

You Will Need:

• a small cardboard box • scissors • cotton wool
• tomato ketchup • the middle finger of your left hand

WHAT YOU DO

1. Cut a small hole in the bottom of the box, just big enough to get your finger through.

2. Fill the box with cotton wool.

3. Once you've done this, cover the cotton wool around the hole with some ketchup.

4. Next, put your finger through the hole and lay your finger in the cotton wool. It looks gruesome, doesn't it?

5. Hold the box so it's resting in the palm of your left hand.

Now it's time to have some fun. Tell a friend that you have a severed finger in a box. Of course, he won't believe you and he'll think it's a fake plastic finger that you've bought in a joke shop. Ask him to touch it. He's sure to grin and grab it, thinking that you're silly for believing he'll fall for such a simple trick.

Of course, the moment he touches it, he'll feel a finger made of real flesh and bone and jump away with a look of absolute terror on his face.

HOW TO WIN A NOBEL PRIZE

Having decided to become the best, the top award to aim for is a Nobel Prize, awarded since 1901 for great achievements in Physics, Chemistry, Medicine, Literature, Economics and Peace.

A Swedish scientist, named Alfred Nobel, gave some of his fortune to be used as prizes for the awards. He had become rich by inventing dynamite. He spent years experimenting and managed to blow up quite a few people – including his younger brother – along the way! Here is your very own step-by-step guide to winning one of these prestigious awards.

EYES ON THE PRIZE

- Work hard at school. Don't worry, this is the boring bit – it gets better from now on.

- Make sure you become a scientist, writer, economist or worker for peace (there's no Nobel Prize for football, unfortunately).

- Now for the tricky bit. You need to do something special. For the science awards, your best bet is to invent or discover something. This should be something useful. A cure for a disease is really good; inventing a clockwork toenail clipper is much less likely to get you noticed. Whatever you invent, try very hard not to blow up any younger brothers during your experiments.

- For the Literature Prize, you need to write some wonderful books. Keep reading regularly to see what your favourite authors are writing about, and get some inspiration from them.

- The Economics Prize is yours if you can come up with new theories about how the world of money works, or should work.

- The best way to win the Nobel Peace Prize is to find a war and stop it. This is quite a tricky thing to do, but probably won't involve as much homework as the other Nobel Prizes you might be aiming for.

WHAT NEXT?

- You have to wait for someone to nominate you. This has to be someone such as a famous scientist or a university professor. Unfortunately you can't just get your best friend to nominate you.

- Sit by the phone. The call comes just before the awards are announced to the world.

- Pack your passport and some warm clothing (the ceremony is in December) and catch a plane to Stockholm in Sweden.

- Collect your award. Each Nobel Prize winner receives a Nobel Prize diploma, a Nobel Prize medal (made of real gold), and prize money (at the time of writing, this was 10,000,000 Swedish Kroner, which is about £800,000).

- Bask in your glory and feel very pleased with yourself.

Of course, if you really want to show off, there's no need to stop at one Nobel Prize. Marie Curie, a Polish scientist, won two Nobel Prizes, her husband won one, her daughter, Irene, won one, and her other daughter's husband won one, too.

HOW TO BEAT THE HOMEWORK BLUES

You get home from school, throw down your school bag and try to get on with having fun for the rest of the day. The problem is, your homework won't let you. Just the thought of it casts a shadow over the evening – you know it has to be done at some point and you know it's going to take such a long time to do.

Well, not anymore. Follow these top homework-busting tips and you'll be free to enjoy the rest of your day in no time.

GET DOWN TO IT

Homework doesn't take nearly as long as you think. It's just that some people make it last a long time. Before they start they tidy up their school bags, sharpen their pencils or organize their desks. In fact, they do lots of things that aren't actually anything to do with the homework. This is because sorting out a school bag and colouring in the front of your homework file feel like work and are much easier than actually doing any real work.

The best homework-busting trick to try is to get your homework out of your bag and do it straight away, with no distractions. You'll be amazed the first time you try it. It'll cut the time you spend doing your homework in half.

HANDY HOMEWORK HINTS

• Don't let your homework lie around all evening waiting for you. Set aside a regular time to do it. This might be as soon as you get home from school, it might be before your evening meal or it might be later in the evening. You're the best person to decide the most effective time for you. Whatever time you decide, make sure you stick to it every time you have homework to do.

• Another useful technique is to reward yourself for finishing your homework. Think of something you really like doing and only allow yourself to do it once you've finished. If you love playing computer games, reward yourself with half an hour on the computer once your homework is completed.

HOW TO UNDERSTAND WHAT A DOG IS SAYING

Although dogs can't actually speak, this doesn't mean you can't understand what they are telling you. Dogs are descended from wolves and are used to being in a close group, called a pack. They need to be able to communicate with other pack members so they can explain what they want, and work out who's in charge.

Most dogs live with humans nowadays and, as far as they are concerned, the people around them are either part of their pack, or are a threat to their pack. So, they will communicate with them just as if they were other dogs and the main method they use to 'speak' is body language.

Opposite is a useful Dog to Human dictionary to help you make sense of your canine friends.

MOVEMENT	MEANING
Putting part of his body on top of yours – for example a paw resting on your leg	I'm the boss
Patting you with his paw	You're the boss
Lying down watching you	You're the boss
Rolling over so you can rub his stomach	You're the boss
Tearing up things while you're out	I'm upset because you left me on my own
Putting his front feet on the floor with his front legs stretched out and his bottom in the air	I want to play
Bright, alert eyes and relaxed lips, or his tongue hanging out	I'm happy
Lying down thumping his tail on the floor	I'm happy
Emitting a continuous, low growl	I'm warning you that I might attack
Teeth bared and snarling	I'm about to attack
Cocking his head to one side	Hmm, that's interesting

HOW TO MAKE A TIME CAPSULE

It may not be possible to travel into the future, but you can still tell someone in the future what life was like in your time. You can do this by creating a time capsule.

A time capsule is a container full of items that represent life today. It is then sealed and buried for someone to discover years from now. Here's how to make one.

You Will Need:

- a large plastic storage box with a lid
- masking tape
- a marker pen
- a selection of items that sum up your life
- sandwich bags

WHAT COULD YOU PUT INSIDE?

Choose what you are going to put in your time capsule to show the person who finds it what life was like for you. Try and select items that show off your own personality as well as more general objects that show what life today is like.

- A letter to whoever discovers your time capsule, explaining who you are, and what you enjoy doing.
- A newspaper article from the day you bury your capsule.
- A copy of your favourite comic.
- A ticket from an exciting event you have been to, such as a great concert.
- Holiday photographs, or pictures of yourself and your friends.
- Anything else that is important to you. This could be trading cards, pictures you have drawn, or pictures from magazines showing what you are interested in.

WHAT YOU DO

1. Using the marker pen, write, 'Do not open until 2050' (or a year of your choice) in large, clear letters on the lid of the box.

2. Wrap each of your chosen items in plastic sandwich bags to keep them extra safe, then close the lid on the box and seal it securely with masking tape.

3. Find a spot in your garden and bury your time capsule ready for someone in the future to find. Make sure you ask your parents for permission before you start making holes in their beautiful flowerbeds.

4. Once you put your time capsule in the ground, it won't be long before you forget about it. To make sure that someone will one day be able to find it, place a reminder somewhere. For example, write instructions for finding it and slip them under a floorboard, or stick them to the wall behind a wardrobe.

HOW TO STOP A NOSEBLEED

It can be quite frightening to suddenly discover blood pouring from your nose. Usually, nosebleeds are neither painful nor dangerous, so there's nothing to worry about. If you find yourself with a nosebleed, stay calm, follow the advice below and the bleeding should soon stop.

- Most people lean backwards when they find they have a nosebleed. Actually, this is the opposite of what you should do. The blood has to flow and if you lean backwards, it is going to go down your throat, which won't be very pleasant. If you have a nosebleed, sit somewhere comfortable and lean forwards.

- Pinch your nose at the point just above your nostrils. This dams the blood in your nose, and blood that isn't moving forms into a solid clot. You need to pinch your nose for at least ten minutes for this to work.

- With your other hand, apply a cold flannel or an ice pack to the side of your nose. Nosebleeds are often caused by the rupturing of tiny blood vessels, and making the area cold will cause these to shrink and the blood will stop flowing.

- When you let go, the nosebleed will most likely have stopped. If it hasn't you're going to have to pinch it again, perhaps for longer this time.

- When the bleeding has stopped, your nose may feel blocked up and you may want to blow it. Don't. If you blow your nose, you will release the blood clot and the bleeding could start again. Avoid any running around or physical games for the next few hours. If the nosebleed doesn't stop after following these instructions, tell your parents and go to the doctors.

HOW TO PLAY THE DIDGERIDOO

The cool kids at school play the guitar, your mum wants you to play the piano, your teacher suggests something else again. Why not ignore them all and learn to play ... the didgeridoo.

The didgeridoo is the instrument famously played by the Australian Aborigines (the earliest inhabitants of Australia), and is one of the world's oldest instruments. It might sound unbelievable, but the didgeridoo is actually made by insects. The instrument is made from a branch from the Eucalyptus tree. Australian termites hollow out the branches of the tree and the Aborigines cut the branch when the thickness of the wood is just right for a didgeridoo.

While you might not have a real didgeridoo to play, you can still practise the technique. Try using the long cardboard tube from a roll of wrapping paper as your makeshift didgeridoo.

The most important part of playing the didgeridoo is mastering the drone. This isn't the same kind of drone that teachers are so good at; it's the name given to the loud, continuous humming sound produced by the didgeridoo.

WHAT YOU DIDGERI-DO

1. Kneel down with your didgeridoo in front of you. Hold it in one hand with the mouthpiece close to your mouth and the other end resting on the floor. Keep your back straight, so that the didgeridoo is at an angle of roughly 45°.

2. Before you try and get any noise out of the instrument, it's important that your lips are properly relaxed. If you try blowing into the didgeridoo with lips that are too tight, you'll end up producing a seriously uncool squeaking sound. Practise blowing with relaxed lips. You will look like you are doing an impression of a horse, and the noise you make should sound like you're blowing a raspberry.

3. Once you've got your lips loose and relaxed, it's time to start making some noise. Position your lips on the didgeridoo so you have a tight seal around the mouthpiece. Blow straight into the mouthpiece, keeping your lips relaxed at all times. If you get this right, you'll hit what is known as the 'sweet spot', and will produce a deep, resonant drone. This drone will be the basis for your music, and you will need to keep it going in one long, continuous sound.

CIRCULAR BREATHING

Now, unless you've got serious lung power, you will certainly run out of breath. So, you need to learn the didgeridoo player's technique of circular breathing. As you're about to get to the end of your long breath, puff some air into your cheeks.

Push the air from your cheeks into the didgeridoo to continue the drone, while taking a deep breath in through your nose.

Now you will be able to start another long exhale into the didgeridoo without having to cause a break in the sound that you're making. Circular breathing can be quite tricky, so don't worry if it takes you lots of practice. If you start to feel light-headed at any point, then take a break for a while and try again later.

MUSIC MAESTRO

Now you should be droning nicely, and you are ready to add some variety to the noise you're making. Form the letter 'D' repeatedly, tapping your tongue against the roof of your mouth while continuing your drone. This is known as the 'kangaroo hop' and will add some rhythm to your music.

If you want to change the pitch of your drone, try loosening and tightening your lips as you blow, while keeping your tongue against the roof of your mouth. This will create a range of different sounds.

HOW TO EAT WITH CHOPSTICKS

Next time you are in a Chinese restaurant, why not leave the knife and fork alone and show off your chopstick skills? The biggest mistake people usually make is to try to pick up their food by moving both chopsticks. If you do this, the food will slip out from between the chopsticks. The trick is to keep one chopstick still and move the other one to meet it. It isn't easy at first, but keep practising and you'll soon be attracting admiring glances from the other diners. Here's how:

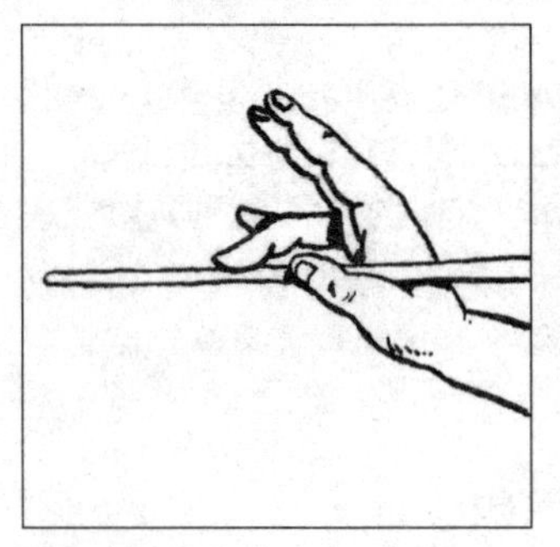

1. To hold the first chopstick, place it so it rests at the base of your thumb and the thinner part rests against your ring finger (the finger between your middle and little fingers). This is the chopstick that stays still when you eat.

2. Hold the other chopstick between your thumb and index finger in the same way you would hold a pencil. The narrow end should be pointing downwards and there should be about 6 cm between the tip of your finger and the thin end of the chopstick. You should now be able to press the ends of the sticks together like a pincer, with this second chopstick on top of the other one.

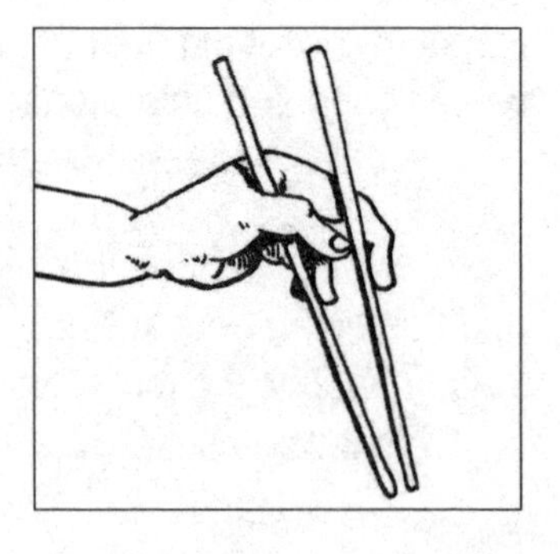

RICE AND EASY

If you are eating rice, it would take a long time to pick up the grains of rice between your chopsticks. This is where technique number two comes in.

Hold the chopsticks in the same way as above, but do this so there is a little bit of space between the two ends. Don't move either of the sticks. All you do now is use the two chopsticks to scoop up the rice. The Chinese don't consider it rude if you pick up your plate or bowl and hold it close to your face when you do this.

Of course, chopsticks shouldn't be used for eating everything. Using your new-found chopstick skills on a bowl of soup or ice cream, for instance, will end messily, no matter how practised you are.

HOW TO MAKE A WATER SLIDE

Summer's arrived and you're sitting in the park under a hot sun wishing you were at a water park. Well, if you can't get there, why not bring the water park to you? It takes no time at all to make a really fun water slide.

You Will Need:

• a large open space, such as a field, park or a large garden • a long roll of plastic sheeting (you will be able to get this from a hardware shop) • a hose pipe or some buckets of water • washing-up liquid

WHAT YOU DO

1. Look carefully at the ground to make sure there are no stones or sharp objects where you are making the slide.

2. Unroll the plastic. Make sure you have got enough space to take a run up to your slide without bumping into anyone.

3. Spray the whole slide with water, either from a hose pipe, or by throwing several buckets of water over it. Squeeze some washing-up liquid along the length of the plastic to give you extra sliding power.

It's now ready to use. Take a good run up and then, without stopping, drop on to the slide in a sitting position, then lie on your back and whizz along the slide. If you're feeling daring, you could try and make it all the way along the slippery slide on your feet, but be warned – it's very tricky to keep your balance. However you tackle your water slide, make sure that there are no obstacles at the end of it so that you land safely.

HOW TO MAKE A COIN GO THROUGH A TABLE

Slamming a coin down on a table so that it looks like it goes straight through is a quick and impressive trick to learn. It's also a trick you can do anywhere as all you need is a coin and a table. The best time to do it, though, is at lunch or dinner when everyone is sitting around a table.

WHAT YOU DO

1. Sit at the table with the coin in your right hand and your left hand resting on your lap.

2. Raise your right hand and slam the coin on the table so your hand is covering it. Slide your hand off the table and make a fist so it looks like you are picking the coin up.

3. When you slide your hand to the edge of the table, let the coin fall into your lap. It is important that you sit with your legs together so the coin doesn't drop onto the floor.

4. Now, raise your right hand, still in a fist. Remember there is no coin in this hand now, although those watching think that there is.

5. While everyone is watching your right hand, pick the coin off your lap with your left hand and hold it under the table at the spot above which your right hand is going to land.

6. Slam your right hand down on the table so that, once again, your hand is flat. At exactly the same time as your right hand lands, use your left hand to hit the underside of the table with the coin. It is this sound of the coin hitting the table that makes the trick work.

7. As everyone watches, raise your right hand so they can see there is no coin on the table or in your hand.

8. Remove your left hand from under the table and show the coin. To the confused audience, it will look as if the coin has gone straight through the table and landed in your left hand.

HOW TO WIN THE TOUR DE FRANCE

The Tour de France is one of the world's toughest races – it's a worthy challenge for any boy who wants to be the best at everything. Over a period of three weeks, the top cyclists in the world race nearly 3,500 kilometres, sometimes cycling more than 200 kilometres in a single day, riding over some of Europe's most fearsome mountains. If you plan to beat them, there are a few things to bear in mind.

1. Don't cheat! The first winner was Maurice Garin in 1903, who received a hero's welcome when he crossed the finish line. The following year, he won again but was stripped of his title when it was discovered he had sneakily taken the train to arrive first.

2. Eat like a horse. In fact, eat like two horses. A cyclist on the Tour uses about three times more energy than an average man. So, a typical breakfast would be two big bowls of cereal, plenty of fruit, a four-egg omelette and a large bowl of pasta.

3. Don't expect a fantastic prize for winning. The winner receives a jersey. The overall winner gets a yellow jersey, the best young rider gets a white one, and the King of the Mountains (the fastest rider up the mountains) receives a red polka-dot jersey. There is also prize money to be had, but the winner usually gives this away to his team-mates.

TOP TRAINING TIPS

It's important to train properly for the Tour de France, or any cycling event that you're planning on tackling. Follow these top tips to be a real cycling superstar:

- Make sure your bike's saddle is at the correct height. You should be able to touch the ground with your foot when you tilt the bike slightly.

- Safe riding is essential. Wear a helmet whenever you are on your bike. A large part of the Tour de France takes place on roads, but while you're training you should never cycle on your own, and always stay away from busy roads. The best and most fun way to cycle safely is to join your local cycling club.

- Don't start by attempting long distances – build up slowly. If you can comfortably cycle three kilometres, try doing five.

- When going on a long ride, drink water regularly. Cycling can cause dehydration, which means your body isn't getting enough liquid.

- Remember that the Tour de France is a race, and if you want to be in with a chance of winning you need to develop speed as well as endurance. Every now and again while you're cycling, try sprinting as fast as you can for 30 seconds.

- Find a nearby hill and practise using your bike's gears. If you use them correctly, you should be able to keep to the same speed as you travel upwards. What goes up must come down, so it's important to practise a downhill technique, too. When cycling downhill, keep your upper body relaxed and start to brake before any bends to avoid your wheels skidding.

HOW TO OPEN A COCONUT

There's nothing that sums up the taste of the tropics as much as cool coconut milk and the wonderful flavour of white coconut. If you should find yourself feeling peckish while on a tropical island paradise, then you need to crack the method for opening a coconut to get at the delicious food inside. Here's how:

1. First, pull off the hairy layer around the outside of the coconut with your fingers.

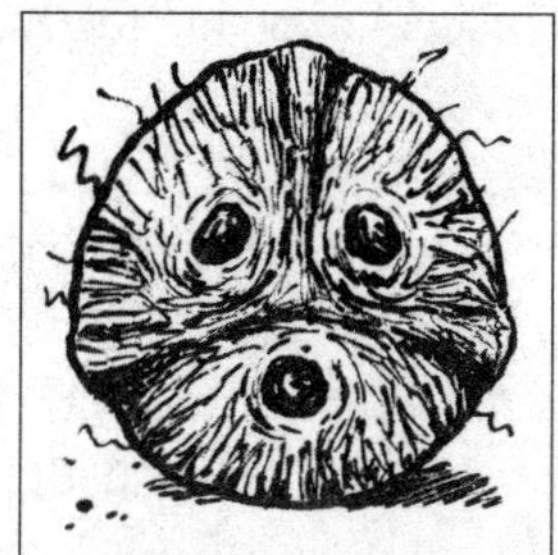

2. Look closely at the coconut. You will see three black spots, each the size of a small coin. These are the coconut's weak spots. Push a sharp stick through two of these holes and hold the coconut over a container to let the milk drain out.

3. There is a line, called a 'seam', running between the top two black spots. Follow this to the middle of the coconut, then form an imaginary line around the fattest part of the middle.

4. Tap the coconut sharply with a rock all the way around this imaginary line. The coconut should soon break apart into two halves.

5. Once your coconut is open, you can carefully cut the white bits away from the shell. Check that they don't smell sour or mouldy, and then pop them into your mouth.

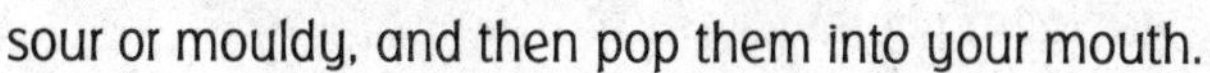

HOW TO MAKE A SCARY COSTUME

There are many occasions that call for a really scary costume, so you should know how to create a terrifying impression easily and very effectively. Vampires, zombies and monsters can all be a bit disturbing, but for true terror nothing beats the Grim Reaper. He appears in his dark robes, carrying his scythe and bringing death to all he chooses to visit. Read on to find out how to transform your nice, handsome self into a being that strikes horror into the bravest soul.

You Will Need:

• white and black face paints • a broom handle
• two pieces of thin card (two flattened cereal packets will do)
• a small can of silver spray paint (ask an adult to buy this for you, or use grey poster paint) • a pen • sticky tape

WHAT YOU DO

1. Flatten each cereal packet and draw the shape of the scythe blade on both of them, making sure that the shapes are exactly the same size. Then cut them out.

2. Lay the shapes on a piece of newspaper so they are facing back to back as shown. Spray the silver paint so it completely covers your scythe shapes. Make sure you are in a well-ventilated area when you do this, and spray the paint at arm's length, away from your face.

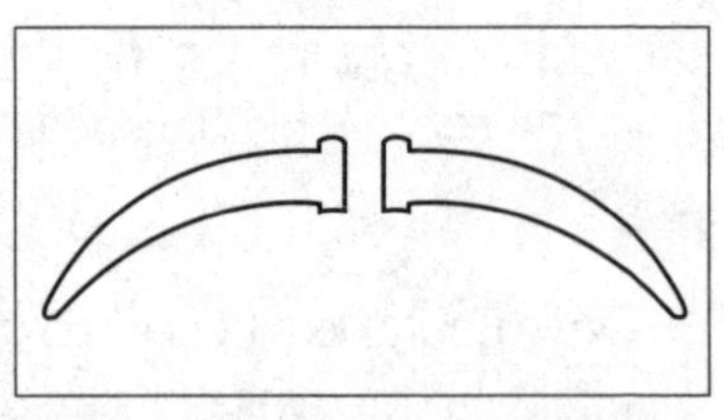

3. Spray paint dries quickly, but make sure it is fully dry. If it's still wet, it will stick to the newspaper. Leave it to dry for about half an hour to make sure.

4. Take the broom handle and tape one of your terrifying scythes to each side of the top of the handle. Use lots of tape so it is fixed securely.

FINISHING TOUCHES

Now you have finished the centrepiece of your costume, it's time to dress the part. The Grim Reaper wears a long, black cloak with a hood. Perhaps you or a member of your family has a black coat you can use. Alternatively, a blanket works well if you place it over your head and shoulders. Put a belt around the waist and a safety pin just under your neck to hold the blanket in place.

Finally, use white face paint to cover your face and hands and use the black face paint to make circles round your eyes and over your lips. Now you're ready to do some serious scaring.

HOW TO THROW A FRISBEE

There are some skills that mark out the cool people from everyone else, and one of these is being able to throw a Frisbee. It is essential you know how to do this so that everyone at the beach or in the park is in no doubt whatsoever that you are one of the cool guys.

There are three things to get right if you are going to do this well – gripping the Frisbee, swinging your arm, and throwing the Frisbee.

Note: The instructions below are for right-handed people. If you are left-handed, simply reverse the left and right instructions.

THE GRIP

Hold the Frisbee with your palm against the rim, your fingers wrapped round the rim and your thumb on top. Your wrist should be curled slightly inwards, towards your body.

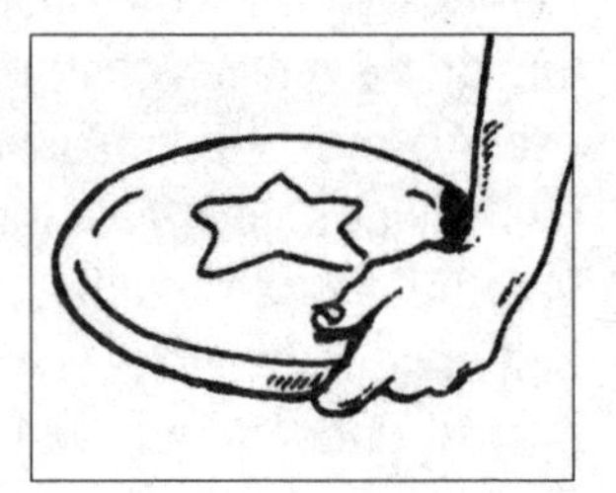

THE SWING

Your arm should be across your body. In other words, hold the Frisbee in your right hand and bring your right arm across your chest so the Frisbee is to the left of your body.

THE THROW

Move your arm away from your body and release the Frisbee when the angle between your arm and your body is about 45°. Release it with a quick snap of the wrist. It is your wrist that is providing the power to make the Frisbee fly.

TOP THROWING TIPS

- Keep looking at the person you are throwing to, not at the Frisbee.
- It is important the Frisbee is level when you release it. It should not tilt down, or to the left or right.
- Your movements should be nice and smooth. There is no need to throw it as hard as you can. The chances are this will just make the Frisbee fly off in the wrong direction.

HOW TO LEARN YOUR NINE TIMES TABLE VERY EASILY

Spending hours memorizing your times tables can be a real drag, but with this simple trick the nine times table will puzzle you no longer. All you need to do is hold out your hands with the palms facing you.

1 x 9: Bend finger number one (the thumb on your left hand). There are nine fingers to the right of this finger, so the answer is 9.

2 x 9: Release your thumb and bend finger number two. There is one finger to the left of the one you have bent down (making one in the tens column) and eight fingers to the right (the units column). So, the answer is one ten and eight units: 18.

3 x 9: Bend finger number three. There are two fingers to the left of the one you have bent down (making two in the tens column) and seven fingers to the right (the units column). So, the answer is two tens and seven units: 27.

4 x 9: Bend finger number four. There are three fingers to the left of the one you have bent down and six fingers to the right, giving an answer of 36.

5 x 9: Bend finger number five. There are four fingers to the left and five to the right, so 5 x 9 is 45.

6 x 9: Bend finger six. There are five fingers to the left and four to the right, so 6 x 9 is 54.

7 x 9: Bending finger seven leaves six fingers to the right and three to the left, making 63.

8 x 9: Bending finger eight gives seven fingers and two fingers, making 72.

9 x 9: Bending finger nine gives eight fingers and one finger, making 81.

10 x 9: Bending the last finger leaves nine fingers to the left and none to the right, so 10 x 9 is 90.

Easy, isn't it? Unfortunately, you've now run out of fingers, so you'll have to learn the last two: 11 x 9 = 99 and 12 x 9 = 108. But, you'll never again have problems with multiplying nine by any number up to ten.

HOW TO SHUFFLE CARDS LIKE A PRO

Shuffling cards is not just about mixing the deck before a game. It's also a great chance to impress your friends with your coolness. Next time you play cards, instead of shuffling in the normal way, why not use the Riffle Shuffle. This looks difficult – which is why it will impress everyone – but only takes a little bit of practice to get right.

WHAT YOU DO

1. Split the pack in half. The cards only need to be split roughly in half, so there's no need to count them out.

2. Take one half in your left hand, holding the top of the half-deck with your thumb and the bottom with your middle finger.

3. Do the same to the other half of the deck with your right hand.

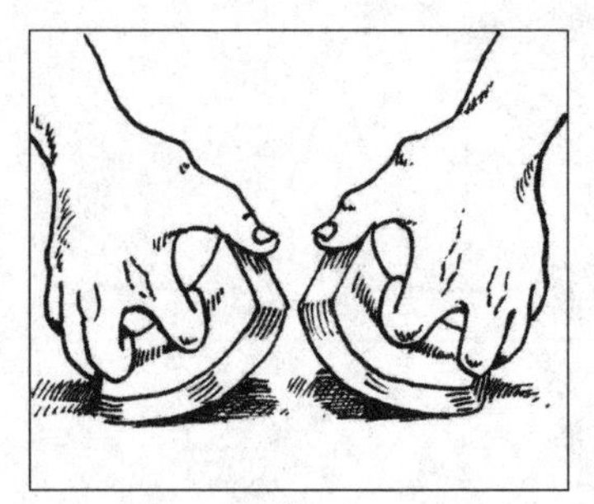

4. Hold the two half-decks upside down and next to each other, just above a table.

5. Push the decks into a curve by pressing the knuckle of your index finger into the back of them. Lean the cards on the table if necessary.

6. The next part takes a little practice to get right. Fire the cards down on to the table, releasing them smoothly by curving your thumb slowly away. The cards should spring down so that, as cards from your left hand land on the table, cards from your right hand interweave with them. This continues until all the cards are on the table and mixed up.

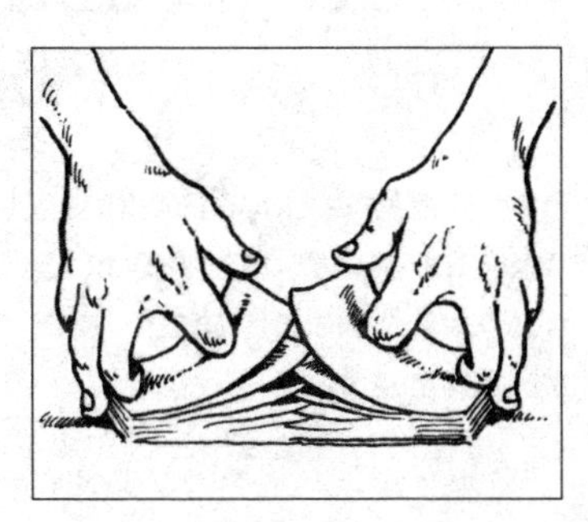

7. Carefully lift up the two half-decks, one in each hand. You could just slide them together into one deck now, but not if you want to look like a real card-shuffling pro. So, push the cards in slightly and then, resting your thumbs on the top of the decks, place your other fingers underneath and bend the decks upwards.

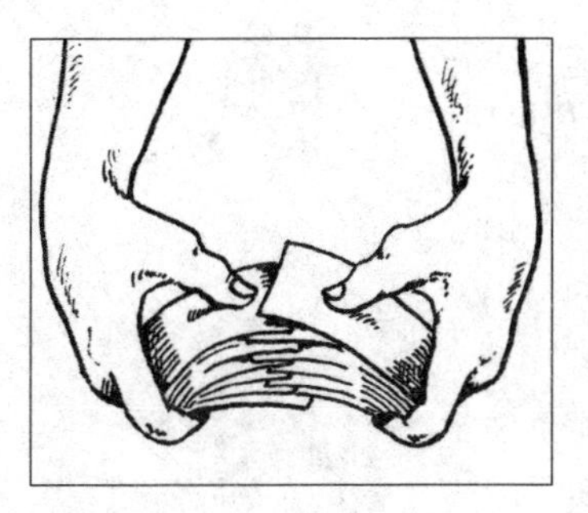

8. Finally, let go with your fingers and push down with your thumbs while pressing your palms inwards. The cards will spring together into one pack.

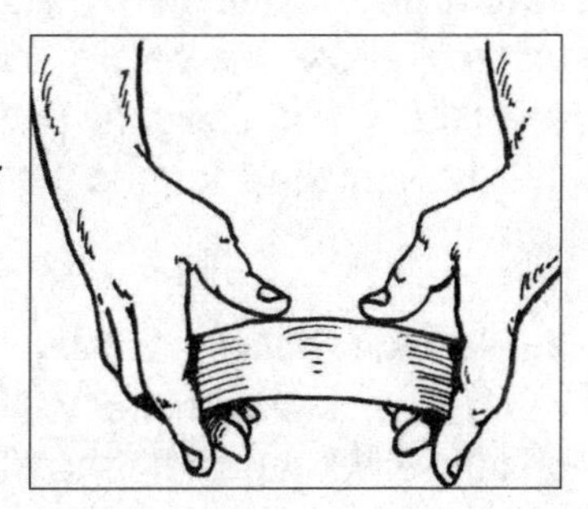

HOW TO CUSTOMIZE YOUR T-SHIRT

However cool your T-shirt is, chances are that someone will have the same one. A great way to make sure you really stand out (and have lots of fun, too) is to create your very own designer shirt.

You Will Need:

• a plain T-shirt • two pieces of thick cardboard • a pencil • a marker pen • scissors • fabric paint • a paintbrush • old newspaper • sticky tape

To make this cool 'crazy face' T-shirt you are going to make a stencil using one of your pieces of cardboard. A stencil is a cut-out shape used to paint your image onto your T-shirt, so when you're finished, the face will be printed onto your T-shirt in one, bright, bold colour.

WHAT YOU DO

1. Take one of your pieces of cardboard and make sure that it is big enough to cover the T-shirt. Using the pencil, draw the shape of the eyes and the mouth onto the card.

2. Fill in the shapes you have drawn using the marker pen, this will give you an idea of what your finished T-shirt will look like.

3. Carefully cut the shape out of the cardboard. Poke the scissors through the centre of the tongue and start from this hole, working outwards to the outline of the mouth and tongue until you have a mouth-shaped hole in the cardboard. Do the same for the eyes, first cutting around the outer black line, and then the inner line. You will be left with two, smaller pieces of cardboard that fit inside the eyes – do not throw these away. Ask an adult to help you if you find this tricky.

4. Place your T-shirt on some sheets of old newspaper and put the other piece of card inside the shirt. This card stops the paint going through to the back of the T-shirt.

5. Put your stencil on top of the T-shirt so the picture is where you want it to be and tape it in place. Make sure you tape the centres of the eyes in place too, using loops of sticky tape.

6. Now, carefully brush the fabric paint onto the T-shirt. By using the stencil, the paint only goes onto the part of the shirt where the cut-out shape is.

7. Leave the stencil taped to the shirt for a couple of hours while the paint dries and then carefully remove it. Your new 'crazy face' T-shirt is now ready to wear.

HOW TO FLIP A PANCAKE

If you fancy a nice, quick snack, have a go at making, flipping and eating a delicious pancake. This recipe is enough to make eight pancakes, so you can share them with your friends.

You Will Need:

• 125 g plain flour • 250 ml milk • an egg • olive oil • a tasty topping • a fantastic flipping technique

WHAT YOU DO

1. Add the flour and milk to a mixing bowl.

2. Crack the egg and pour this into the bowl. When you've done this, mix the ingredients together with a whisk until the mixture (called 'batter') is smooth and has no lumps.

3. Heat about a teaspoonful of oil in a frying pan and then tilt the pan and move it in a circular motion so a thin layer of oil covers the bottom of the pan.

4. Using a ladle, pour a small amount of batter into the middle of the pan. Repeat the motion you made with the oil to spread a thin layer of batter over the whole pan.

5. Cook the pancake on a low-to-medium heat until the batter is firm.

FLIPPING MARVELLOUS

Shake the frying pan to make sure the pancake is loose. If it's sticking to the pan, ease it up gently with a spatula. The pancake needs to be loose so you get a good takeoff.

Hold the pan loosely in your hand. Give it a quick, sharp flick upwards. Start with the pan pointing slightly downwards and use a scooping motion to make sure the pancake turns over in the air.

Catch the pancake in your frying pan and let it cook for a minute on the other side.

TOP TOPPING TIPS

You can add whatever you like to your finished pancake, but here are some tasty topping ideas to get you started:

Lemon and sugar: The classic.
Maple syrup: A sweet treat.
Fruit and ice cream: Nutritious and delicious.
Ham and cheese: Sensationally savoury.
Tomato and mushroom: A veggie delight.

HOW TO KEEP A NEW YEAR'S RESOLUTION

A new year means a new start, so it's a time when people make their New Year's Resolutions. These often include promising to do something to improve themselves or trying to get rid of a bad habit.

Here are some tips to make sure your resolution lasts the whole year.

DO plan. It's no good just saying you are going to do something – you need to plan how you will do it. Write your plan down to help yourself stick to it.

DON'T rush into it. You will only keep your resolution if it's important to you. Think very carefully about how you would like to improve your life and use that to help you decide on your resolution. It's very easy to make a resolution, but to keep one it has to be something you really want to achieve.

DO reward yourself. If you have promised to keep your room tidy, save a little bit of your pocket money each week that you tidy your room, and buy yourself a present at the end of the month.

DO tell everyone. You might have promised to help with the housework more often, so tell your parents and they'll keep reminding you. It might be that you and your friends have made similar resolutions, so by telling each other what you're planning to achieve you'll be able to help each other make your resolutions last.

DON'T overstretch yourself. If you are worried that you eat too many sweets, don't promise to give them up forever. Aim to cut down, perhaps only having sweets at the weekend.

DON'T give up at the first failure. There may be times when you do not manage to keep your resolution. For example, you may have promised to do your homework on time, but forgot to do so on a particular day. This isn't an excuse to give up on your resolution. Just accept you will make the odd mistake and carry on trying.

HOW TO FLY A KITE

It flies, it soars, it dives, and all the time you are the one in control. If you're wondering what to spend your pocket money on, or what to ask your parents for on your birthday, why not get a kite? They are fantastic fun, can be flown wherever there's a bit of open space, and they are easy to fly. Grab a friend, follow these few instructions and your kite will soon be high in the air.

HIGH FLYER

1. For your kite to fly, you need wind. It doesn't have to be a strong wind, but a decent breeze is essential.

2. Face into the oncoming wind, then turn your back on it.

3. Keep hold of the spool of string. Ask your kite-flying partner to take the kite and walk at least 15 metres away from you and then to stand holding the kite loosely in his hands. He should walk in the same direction as you are facing.

4. Pull the string so it is tight and wait for a good gust of wind.

5. Ask your partner to hold the kite above his head, then pull on the string so that the kite leaves your partner's hands and rises in the air.

6. Once your kite is flying, you can gradually unwind your spool to let out more string so the kite can climb higher and higher.

7. If there is a drop in the wind and it starts to fall, pull the line tight by winding the string in or by running away from the kite.

8. To land your kite, simply walk towards it while winding in the string.

DON'T FLY YOUR KITE ...

• during bad weather • near electric cables, telephone lines or trees • over people, in case it falls on them • near roads

If you follow these four don'ts, you'll be sure to keep yourself, your kite, and everybody else safe.

HOW TO PULL A COIN FROM SOMEONE'S EAR

This is a trick that every magician should know. With some simple hand movements you'll be able to convince your friend that you have produced a coin from his ear. Here's how to do it.

1. Take a coin in your right hand and show it to your friend. Make sure you also show them that your other hand is empty.

2. Turn your right hand over, and pretend to transfer the coin from your right hand into your left one. Close your left fist around the imaginary coin, and move your right hand (which still has the coin in it) down by your side.

3. Ask your friend to blow on your left hand, then open it to show that the coin has magically vanished.

4. Bring your right arm up and place your hand behind your friend's ear.

5. In one fluid motion, slide the coin from the palm of your right hand into your fingertips, and bring the coin out from behind your friend's ear. Magic!

HOW TO READ BODY LANGUAGE

Think about how many things you say in an average day. It may amaze you to know that you communicate even more through body language than through speech.

Understanding body language helps us discover what people really mean and how they really feel. Someone might say one thing, but body language signals may tell a different story. We all know a smile means happiness or friendliness, and crying means sadness, but here are some less well-known signals to look out for.

DECISIONS, DECISIONS

- If a person is stroking his chin, he is thinking about something and trying to make a decision.
- If he is tugging his ear, it means he can't make his mind up.
- If you try to help by making a suggestion and he pinches his nose and closes his eyes, it means he doesn't think it is a good idea.

LIAR! LIAR!

Tell-tale signs of lying can be difficult to spot, but clues someone may be lying to you include the person:

- Looking away to the left

- Covering his mouth with his hand while speaking
- Rubbing his nose
- Turning away from you

I'M THE BOSS

- If someone leans back and puts his hands behind his head, he thinks he is in control.
- He might also use his hands to make a steeple shape to show he's in charge.
- Someone standing with his hands on his hips means he feels ready to take on anything. Be careful, though, as it can also be a sign of aggression.

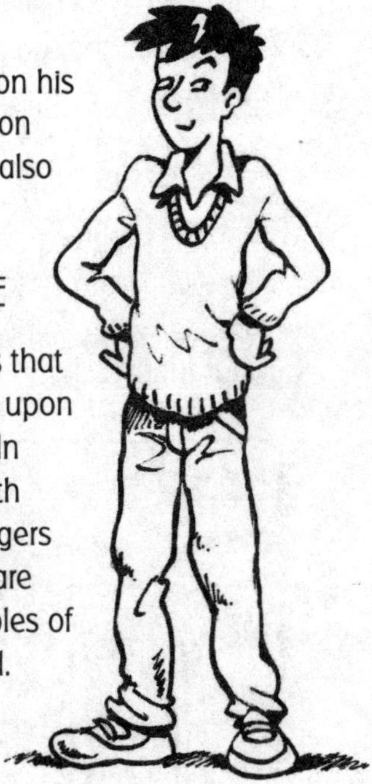

WORLD-WIDE BODY LANGUAGE

Another important point to remember is that body language can change depending upon which country of the world you are in. In Chile, showing someone your hand with your palm facing upwards and your fingers spread out means you think that they are stupid, and in Thailand, showing the soles of your feet is seen to be very rude indeed. So, as well as learning to read the body language of those around you, you should always check your own body language to make sure you're not sending out the wrong signals.

HOW TO TRAIN YOUR GOLDFISH TO PLAY FOOTBALL

A lot of people are unkind about goldfish, saying they only remember things for three seconds and that they are not very intelligent. Well, here's how to prove them wrong by teaching your goldfish to be a soccer star.

First, prepare your pitch. Buy green pebbles for the bottom of your goldfish's bowl or tank from your local pet shop. Next, make a simple goal using three small sticks taped together. Don't use a net, though – you don't want your goldfish getting tangled up.

TRAINING

Have you ever noticed that whenever you go near the fish tank, the fish swim to the surface? This is because they know they might be fed when someone comes near the tank. It is this behaviour that will help you train them.

- Put a small ball in the tank – light enough for the fish to be able to move but heavy enough to sink in the water.

- Now, wait. Sooner or later, the fish will nudge the ball. When this happens, give a tiny piece of food to the fish.

- Wait until the fish moves the ball again and drop in another piece of food. If you do this often enough, the fish will learn that nudging the ball leads to being fed and will start to move the ball around. You will need to be patient with your fish as it does take time to learn. It will probably take a couple of training sessions a day for two to three weeks to turn your goldfish into a footballing legend.

- It is very important not to overfeed the fish. Don't give it more than its usual daily allowance and stop feeding the fish if it doesn't swim up and eat the food immediately.

Congratulations! You are now a successful goldfish trainer. You'll be able to move on to dolphins next.

HOW TO DRAW A MURAL

A mural is a large picture painted straight onto a wall. If you decide to draw one, make sure you ask permission before you start. Here's a simple method that will have you drawing a marvellous mural in no time.

You Will Need:

• a picture or photograph • paintbrushes • various colours of emulsion paint • a soft lead pencil • a sheet of tracing paper • a ruler • a wall • sheets of old newspaper

WHAT YOU DO

1. Find a picture you would like to turn into a mural. It could be a photograph, or a drawing you've done yourself. Place a sheet of tracing paper over the top of the image to protect it.

2. You are going to draw a grid over it. Using a ruler, draw a pencil line on the tracing paper down the centre of the picture. Then draw a line across the centre of the picture. You now have four boxes, each the same size.

3. Draw a line down the middle of the top left-hand box and across the centre of it. Repeat this for all four boxes, making a grid of 16 equal-sized boxes.

4. Draw a large box on the wall using a soft lead pencil. This box will contain 16 larger boxes. For example, if your picture is 15 cm long and 10 cm wide, you could draw a box that's 150 cm long and 100 cm wide.

5. Divide this box into 16 smaller boxes using the same method as before. You now have a larger grid to match the one you drew on your picture.

6. Draw the outline of the mural using the boxes as a guide. Copy the bit of the picture that is in the bottom left box into the bottom left box on the wall, and continue until the outline is complete.

7. Put some old newspapers on the floor so paint doesn't drip on to it, and begin painting your mural masterpiece.

HOW TO TALK LIKE A PIRATE

There are many reasons you might want to talk like a pirate – maybe you've decided that piracy is the perfect career path for you, you might want to liven up a family boat trip, or perhaps some of your best friends are buccaneers. Whatever the reason, this guide to pirate lingo should give you most of what you need to know to become a true swashbuckling speaker.

INSULTS

It is important to know these, as pirates spend a lot of time insulting people.

Landlubber – Anyone who isn't a pirate or sailor.

Scurvy Knave – Scurvy was an illness pirates got because they didn't have fresh fruit at sea. You don't have to make sure someone has scurvy before using this insult, though – it'll do for anybody.

Lily-Livered – Cowardly.

EXCLAMATIONS

Pirate exclamations are useful as you can shout them out at any time you want.

Shiver Me Timbers! – Timbers are the wooden beams on a sailing ship. Pirates shout this phrase when they're surprised or annoyed – pretty much any time really.

There She Blows! – Usually used when a whale is spotted, but you shouldn't feel limited to whale watching. Use it whenever you like, for example when you see the school bus arriving, when your mum arrives home from work, or when your dinner is ready.

THREATS

When pirates are not insulting people, they are usually threatening them. Here are a few useful threats to add to your pirate vocabulary:

I'll Split Your Gizzard – I bet you didn't know you had a gizzard, did you? Or that it can be split? Well, you have, and it can, and it's not very nice.

Marooning – A pirate punishment was to leave people on uninhabited islands, known as 'marooning'. Unless your friends have read this book, they may not know what it means, so you can threaten to maroon them even if you don't have a desert island handy.

Keel-Hauling – Keel-hauling was horrible. Pirates used to tie someone to a rope, throw them overboard and pull them along underneath the boat. This was very painful indeed as their skin would be ripped off by the barnacles on the bottom of the boat. Threatening to keel-haul someone should be reserved for really, really serious punishments.

OTHER USEFUL WORDS AND PHRASES

Me Hearties – My friends.
Jolly Roger – The pirate flag; a black flag with a white skull and crossbones.
Ahoy! – Hello!
Ye – You. For example, 'I'll split your gizzard, ye scurvy knave, if I don't keel-haul ye first.'
Be – Use this instead of 'am', 'is' and 'are'. For example, 'I be a true pirate and ye be a lily-livered landlubber.'

HOW TO PLAY 'FIND THE LADY'

'Find the Lady' is guaranteed to catch your friends out. This is a trick that uses 'sleight of hand', which means you use skilful hand movements to confuse the audience.

1. Take a pack of playing cards and remove two kings and one queen. The queen is the 'Lady' the audience has to find. To help you perform this trick, bend the three cards slightly down the middle, so that the backs curve into a gentle 'upside-down-V' shape.

2. Lay the cards out face down on the table, and pick each one up to show your audience what is on them.

3. Pick up one of the kings and hold it in your right hand, with your thumb at the bottom and your middle finger at the top. Don't grip the card too tightly.

4. Next, pick up the queen in your right hand and hold it in front of the king with your thumb at the bottom and your ring finger at the top.

5. Hold the second king in your left hand in the same way as the first king, with your thumb at the bottom of the card and your middle finger at the top.

6. This is where it gets tricky. Flick your right hand sharply down towards the table, and release your middle finger as you do so, so that the king is thrown face down onto the table. It will take some practice to do this smoothly, but once you've cracked it, it will look as though it is the bottom card – the queen – that has landed on the table, not the king.

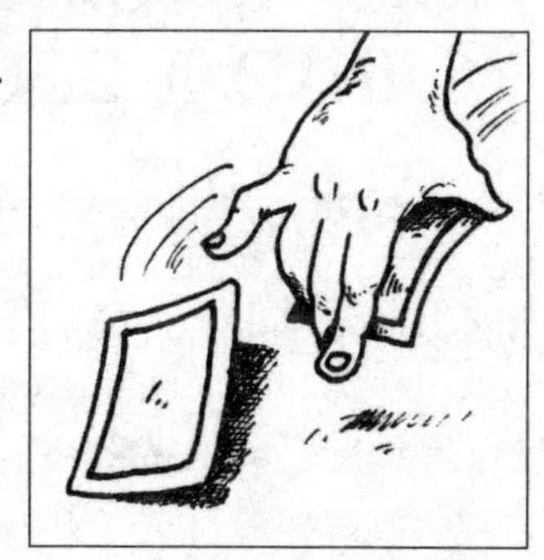

7. With your left hand, put the king to the right of the king lying on the table.

8. With your right hand, put the queen on the left of the king, so the queen will actually be on the left, but the audience will think that she's in the middle.

9. Keep your eye on the king in the middle, and slowly shuffle the cards around, making sure that the king ends up back in the middle where he started.

10. Ask the person watching to 'Find the Lady'. He will point to the card in the middle, thinking this is the queen. Turn the card over to reveal that it is the king and watch his mouth drop open in surprise.

HOW TO TURN YOUR BEDROOM INTO A COOL CRASH PAD

A wall montage is guaranteed to up the 'cool factor' of your bedroom, as it's totally unique to your personality. A montage is a collage of photographs, pictures, souvenirs, and anything else you can think of, that grows over time until it covers a whole wall of your bedroom.

If you want to give your room a montage makeover, here are some top tips.

MONTAGE MAGIC

- Select an area of the wall for your montage. Cover it with brown paper or wrapping paper, so that if there are any gaps in your montage you won't see the wall underneath.

- Choose a theme. Your montage could be based on a hobby or interest of yours, or you could use it as a journal, adding things that remind you of special moments in your life.

- Decide on where you want your montage to start. It could begin in the middle of the wall and grow outwards, or it could start at the bottom and grow upwards.

WHAT TO USE?

Try to use as many different things in your montage as you can, and stick them onto the backing paper with sticky tack. Here are a few ideas:

- You could use photographs. Add to them by having captions coming out of people's mouths, or by cutting and mixing the photos.

- Collect pictures from newspapers, magazines and comics. Just cut out the parts you want.

- Use real objects to give a 3-D effect. For example, you could add old CDs to a music montage. For a sport montage, why not add a rosette in your team's colours?

There's absolutely no limit to what you can use: flattened cola cans, old football shirts, birthday cards, food labels, stickers, graffiti ... the only limits are your own imagination.

HOW TO TAME A LION

Cats are usually affectionate animals that make great pets, but if you're planning on becoming a lion tamer you have to be a bit careful. The pussy cat you'll be dealing with is over a metre tall, weighs 200 kg and has teeth that could tear your head off! The three vital skills a lion tamer needs are caution, bravery and patience. Here's how to teach your lion to do a trick.

JUMPING THROUGH HOOPS

- It is very important that the lion trusts you. Lion tamers often raise their lions from cubs, which gives them a strong bond.

- You are going to teach the lion to respond to a signal. Put a hoop in front of the lion with a toy or bright object on the other side of it. Step back and click your fingers.

- At this point, the lion doesn't know what you are trying to do. If it does step through the hoop to investigate the object on the other side, reward it immediately with some food.

- Keep doing this exercise, and every time the lion steps through the hoop, give a food reward. You will soon find that the lion will step through the hoop when you click your fingers even when the toy is not there.

HOW TO BLUFF AT CARDS

Bluffing means sneakily convincing other players in a card game that you are telling the truth, when really you're telling big fat lies. A good bluffer is a master at keeping a straight face. This is sometimes called a 'poker face' because it is often used by poker players who don't want to give anything away with their facial expressions.

BLUFFING PRACTICE

'Bluff' is a game where, to win, you need to be the first player to get rid of all his cards. The only way to do this is to bluff the other players into thinking you are telling the truth.

You Will Need:

• a pack of playing cards • at least 3 other players (the more players you have, the more fun the game is)

HOW TO PLAY

1. Deal the cards out among the players until all 52 cards have been dealt as evenly as possible.

2. Each player looks at their cards but doesn't let anyone else see them.

3. The player to the left of the dealer starts. He has to get rid of any aces he has by putting them face down in the middle of the table. For example, he may have one ace and so should say, 'One ace' and put this down. However, to get rid of his cards more quickly, he might pretend to have more. He could say, 'Two aces' and put two cards down even if they are not aces. He could even say 'Three aces' and put three cards down, or 'Four aces' and put four down (there are only four of any type of card, so he cannot say more than this).

4. The other players have to decide whether the player who has just put his cards down is bluffing or telling the truth about the cards he has put down. If anyone thinks he is fibbing, they shout, 'Bluff.'

5. If this happens, the player accused of bluffing has to show the cards he has put down. If he is bluffing, he has to pick up all the cards in the middle of the table. If he isn't, then the person who wrongly accused him has to pick the cards up.

6. Each player takes a turn, moving clockwise round the table. After aces, put down the number two cards, then the number three cards, and so on, all the way to number ten. Then the jacks are put down, followed by the queens and, finally, the kings.

7. If you do not have any cards of a particular number, then you can say, 'Pass', or sneakily bluff by playing one or more cards.

The winner is the first person to get rid of all their cards. Be careful, though. You can still be challenged on your last card and, if you are bluffing, you will have to pick up all the cards in the middle.

HOW TO MAKE A BOTTLE ORCHESTRA

A few empty bottles, some water and a teaspoon may not sound like much, but with your talent, they can sound wonderful. Follow these steps and you'll be making music in no time.

SETTING UP YOUR ORCHESTRA

- Find six empty glass bottles. It helps if they are all the same size. Milk bottles are perfect for transforming into an orchestra.
- Fill the bottles with water, but put a different amount in each one. Only put a small amount – a couple of centimetres – in the first bottle. Put a bit more in the next bottle and so on until all six bottles have water in. Make sure that you leave a gap at the top of all of the bottles, even the fullest one.
- Line the bottles up in order. Put the one with the least water at one end and the one with the most at the other end.

- When you tap the side of the bottles gently with a teaspoon, each one will make a different sound. This is because the sound is travelling through different amounts of water. The less water in the bottle, the higher the sound will be.

You are now ready to play that most famous of tunes, *Twinkle, Twinkle, Little Star*. The bottle with the most amount of water in is bottle one. The next bottle is two and so on. Bottle six will be the one with the least water in it. Here's how to play it. The numbers underneath each word of the song represent which bottle you should tap in your orchestra.

TWINKLE, TWINKLE, LITTLE STAR

Twin-kle Twin-kle lit-tle star
1 1 5 5 6 6 5
How I won-der what you are
4 4 3 3 2 2 1
Up a-bove the world so high
5 5 4 4 3 3 2
Like a dia-mond in the sky
5 5 4 4 3 3 2
Twin-kle Twin-kle lit-tle star
1 1 5 5 6 6 5
How I won-der what you are.
4 4 3 3 2 2 1

Top Tip. To make your bottle orchestra really stand out, add a few drops of differently coloured food colouring to each bottle of water.

HOW TO BEAT YOUR FRIENDS IN A TRIAL OF STRENGTH

If any of your friends think they are really strong, you can prove your superior strength with this simple test.

EGG-STRA STRONG

First, ask your friend if he thinks he can break an egg with his bare hands. Of course, he will say, 'Yes'.

Next, ask him to take the egg in one hand, wrap his fingers evenly around it and squeeze it as hard as he can. To his amazement, he will find that the egg is indestructible. This is because, although eggs can be easily broken by hitting them, they are actually designed to take quite a bit of squeezing. If this wasn't the case, they would break when they were being laid.

Now it's your turn. The trick is to make sure that you are wearing a ring. One squeeze and you've got a broken egg.

When you press the eggshell, all the pressure is on one point – the ring. When your friend tried, the pressure was evenly spread out all around the egg.

HOW TO SHINE ON PARADE

'Fall in! Attention! Right, you useless bunch, those boots need to be so shiny you can see your face in them! Understand, Soldier? Or you'll be peeling potatoes for the next three weeks.'

As you can see, it's very important to look your best on parade. This is especially true of your leather boots. Parade-ground sergeants have a real thing about shiny boots. If you arrive on parade without them well-polished, you're in big trouble.

To make sure you don't end up peeling huge piles of potatoes, whitewashing stones or spending night after night on guard duty, here's how to get a real 'spit and shine' polish.

You Will Need:

• a pair of leather boots • two soft cloths • shoe polish • water

TIME TO SHINE

1. Put one hand inside the boot and, with the other hand, use one of the cloths to spread plenty of polish over your boot. When you've done this, leave it to dry for at least five minutes.

2. Wrap the cloth around your index finger (the one next to your thumb) and dip your finger and the cloth in water.

3. Rub the boot with the damp cloth. Do this by making your finger go round and round in small circles. After a while, the polish on it will start to shine.

4. Dip your finger and the cloth into the polish again and apply another thin layer of polish to the boot. Don't use much polish this time. Use the same circular motion as you did before and keep rubbing until the boot shines even more.

5. Repeat this two or three more times until the boot is highly polished, then use a clean, dry cloth to give a final shine.

6. Check to make sure you can see your face reflected in the polish and, if so, you are ready to go on parade.

Top Tip. This is called a 'spit and shine' polish, because a lot of soldiers don't bother using water. They just spit on the cloth instead.

HOW TO BECOME A RAPPING SENSATION

To become a true rap sensation you need to learn to 'freestyle'. Freestyling is when rappers make up raps as they go along. They might do this by themselves, they might do it with a partner, or they might do it as a 'rap battle' where two rappers take turns trying to out-rap each other. Freestyle rapping is amazing to listen to and really impresses an audience.

Follow these top tips and you can become a truly sensational freestyle rapper.

TIME TO RHYME

- The key to rapping is making up rhymes. Usually, each pair of lines rhyme. This is the part that takes practice. You can help yourself by having some prepared (for example, whenever you rap about school, remember that it rhymes with 'cool', or if you're rapping about a boy, you have easy rhymes with 'toy', 'joy' or 'annoy'.). Pre-plan words that rhyme with your name, your town or other words you know you will use in your raps.

- The best way, though, is to think ahead. If you say the line: 'My rapping is so good', you should immediately be thinking about what rhymes with 'good' – then you could add the line, 'The best in the 'hood' or, 'And that's understood.'

- Try to end your lines with words that are easy to rhyme. If you say, 'The sun is yellow', your next line could end with 'fellow', 'hello' or 'mellow'. However, if you say,'The sun is orange', you will have problems finding a rhyme, because there are no common words that rhyme with orange.

- It's important that your rap has rhythm as well as rhyme. Try and keep each line the same length to give your rap a distinct beat.

- If you make a mistake or stumble over your words, just keep going. The same applies if your line doesn't rhyme. As long as you keep the rap going, people won't really notice.

- Try putting a rap group, called a 'cipher', together with your friends. This makes rapping a bit easier because you can be thinking of your lines while your friends rap.

Remember, learning how to rap is all about practice, practice and more practice. Keep at it, and you'll soon be looking and sounding like a cool rapper. Once you've practised, you're ready to show your classmates just how good you are:

'When I go to school
They all think I'm cool
And the reason you see
Is the Boys' Book 3
It's taught me all I know
Like how to ride the rodeo
And how to rap like a pro!'

HOW TO AVOID SEASICKNESS

Up and down! Side to side! You thought your Caribbean cruise would be the holiday of a lifetime, but instead you're feeling rotten. You've been hit by the traveller's curse: seasickness. When you board a ship, you are moving into a world where nothing stays still, which confuses your brain and body and can make you feel ill.

Until you've been on a sea voyage, you won't know whether you suffer from seasickness or not. However, there are things you can do to help avoid seasickness or to get over it quickly if you become unwell.

- Until you have been at sea for a few hours, you should avoid going below deck. Spend as much time as possible gazing out at the horizon, where the water meets the sky. The horizon is a fixed point, so looking out at it helps your brain get used to being at sea.

- If you do feel unwell, it can help to lie down, but do not lie down in your cabin. Find a comfortable deckchair and lie on deck. Make sure somebody stays with you.

- If you are on a cruise, you will be tempted by all sorts of wonderful, exotic food. Try not to give into temptation during your first day. Eat lightly and eat familiar food.

- If you do get seasick, you will get better. Once at sea, your brain and body will get used to the movement of the ship.

Top Tip. Many experienced travellers say ginger is a good remedy for seasickness. Why not take some ginger biscuits with you when you board?

HOW TO 'SPIKE' A VOLLEYBALL

Spiking a volleyball is the most powerful shot in the game. Done correctly, it's sure to win the point for your team. Spiking a ball means jumping up close to the net and hitting the ball powerfully down into the opponent's side of the court. Here's how to do it.

1. Stand on the attack line that runs a few feet in front of the net and watch the 'setter' – this is the person who is going to pass the ball to you so you can hit it over the net.

2. Take your run up. You will probably need to take three steps to reach the net from the attack line.

3. Jump, and as you do so, throw both arms up above your head. This will give extra power to your jump. Time your takeoff so you hit the ball at the top of the jump.

4. If you are right-handed, pull your right arm back so your elbow is nice and high. Keep your hand close to your head. Your hand should be open with the palm facing upwards.

5. Bring your right hand forwards and hit the top of the ball with the bottom of your palm.

6. Snap your wrist downwards as you hit the ball to spike it into your opponent's side of the court.

HOW TO BE A SUPERSTAR CHARITY FUNDRAISER

Raising money for charity should be easy – after all, everyone likes to support a good cause. However, with so many good causes and so many people trying to raise money, you need to work hard to attract people's attention.

CAREFUL PLANNING

- Your first task is to decide what you will raise money for. This could be a local organization, medical research or helping people in poorer countries.

- Next, decide how to raise the money. One of the best ways is through sponsorship, where people pay you to complete an activity.

- If you decide on a sponsored event, you need to choose what it will be. Fundraising is more effective and much more fun if you do it with friends, so why not organize a sponsored swim at your local pool, for instance?

ORGANIZING THE SWIM

Before you start, you should ask permission from the swimming pool's manager, and make sure that a lifeguard can be present at all times during your swimming event. Ask an adult to help out with the organizing, and oversee your swim.

Set your sponsorship target. The more challenging it is, the more likely people are to give you money. For example, you could do a five kilometre swim. Don't worry if you can't swim this far, you can make it a team effort. Find out the length of the pool. If it's 33 metres, which many public pools are, then 152 lengths of the pool make up five kilometres. If there are 12 swimmers, that's 13 lengths each. If two people swim at a time, everyone gets a rest while waiting for their next turn.

Design sponsorship forms, so that everyone taking part can ask people to sponsor them. The forms should include details of the event, a column for people's names and a column for the amount of money they are giving.

Give all the swimmers an information sheet for the day with the time, date and meeting place. It should also include what people need to bring with them (such as a swimming costume, towel and snacks), and a swimming rota so everyone understands how the day will work.

Once you've finished and had a well-earned rest, you and your friends need to collect the money and decide how you will give it to the organization you are supporting. You may be able to deliver it in person to a local representative, or you might need to send it to the organization. Ask an adult to help you with this.

HOW TO RAISE SOMEONE UP USING 'FINGER POWER'

How strong are your friends? Strong enough to lift you off the ground using only their fingers? No? Well, follow these instructions and you will be amazed by your mates' incredible, superhuman strength.

WHAT YOU DO

You need four friends to lift you using their 'power fingers'. Sit on a chair without arms, such as a school chair. Sit very still and stay relaxed.

Two of your friends should stand behind the chair, the third should stand at the right-hand side of the chair and the fourth at the left-hand side.

Ask one of your friends to place his left hand on top of your head. Your three other friends should then place their left hands on top of his. Ask your friends to do the same with their right hands so that all eight hands are resting on your head.

All four lifters now need to concentrate. While thinking about raising you into the air, they should chant the following aloud 20 times: 'Light as a feather! Stiff as a board!'

The lifters should now remove their hands and then each press their left and right hands together, with both their index fingers sticking out and the others clasped round each other, as shown here.

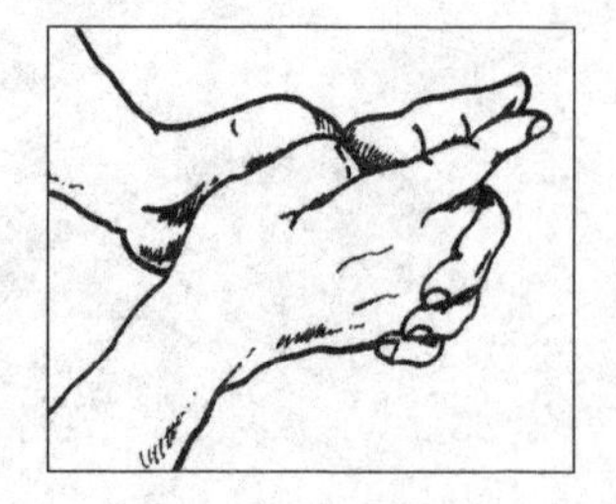

The two people at either side of the chair put these two fingers under each of your knees. The two people standing behind the chair place their fingers under your armpits.

Count to three out loud. When you call out 'three', everybody should lift upwards with their fingers. Incredibly, you will lift up as if you really were as light as a feather. Your friends will be able to lift you quite high, but make sure they let you down again carefully and gently.

Top Tip. Quite often, it takes two or three goes to get this to work properly. If it does not work first time, remember to start again from the beginning and repeat the chanting.

HOW TO BECOME A ROCK 'N' ROLL DRUMMING LEGEND

There's no doubt about it, the drums are great fun to play. It takes practice and skill to master playing the drums, so here are some simple exercises to set you on the path to rock-and-roll-stardom.

GOT RHYTHM?

Pat yourself on the top of your head with an up and down movement, while using your other hand to rub your stomach in circles. Not easy, is it? Drumming is all about doing different things with different parts of your body, and it takes quite a while to be able to do this well.

The next exercise is a lot more challenging. Try it and see how well you do.

Tap a finger of your left hand on the table with a regular rhythm. Every other time it hits the table, hit the table at the same time with a finger of your right hand. The rhythm should go: Left ... Left and Right ... Left ... Left and Right ... Left ....

Got the hang of it? Excellent. Now, repeat the exercise, but every fourth beat, stamp on the floor with your right foot. The rhythm should now go: Left ... Left and Right ... Left ... Left and Right and Right Foot ... and so on.

If you have managed to get this far, you're doing brilliantly. You are taking your first steps on the journey to being a rock 'n' roll drumming legend. Don't relax just yet, though. There is one more step.

Repeat the exercise, but on the second beat and every four beats after that, stamp on the floor with your left foot. The final, complete rhythm should now go:

Left Hand
Left Hand, Right Hand, Left Foot
Left Hand
Left Hand, Right Hand, Right Foot.
Left Hand
Left Hand, Right Hand, Left Foot
Left Hand
Left Hand, Right Hand, Right Foot.

If you've got this far successfully, you've really got the beat. So sign up for lessons at your local music school, start saving up for a drum kit, grow your hair and get drumming!

HOW TO EAT SPAGHETTI WITH STYLE

You're staring out of the window of an Italian restaurant. A delicious plate of spaghetti is in front of you and you're starving. You push a small amount of the pasta into your mouth, the rest hangs down in front of you, smearing tomato sauce all over your chin and your clean, white shirt. At that moment your classmates troop past looking in. Nightmare.

Spaghetti is one of the trickiest foods to eat without making a mess. So you need to be prepared.

SPAGHETTI SKILLS

- You only need a fork to eat spaghetti – not a fork and spoon, or a fork and fingers – just a plain, simple fork.
- Never use a knife to cut the spaghetti up into smaller pieces.
- Clear a space near the edge of your dish – you'll need it later.
- Take your fork and stick it into the middle of the pasta. Don't stick it in too far as you don't want to pick up too much.

Now, press the prongs of the fork against the plate in the space that you have just cleared.

- Twist the fork round and round until the pasta is wound completely round it. There shouldn't be any bits hanging down. If there are, lower your fork, scrape the pasta off against the plate, and try again with a smaller amount of spaghetti.

HOW TO NAVIGATE BY THE STARS

The sky above you is dark and full of twinkling stars. It's certainly very beautiful, but did you know that the night sky also works as a giant compass? Because the stars' positions relating to each other always stay the same, people can use them to find their way in the dark. Sailors out on the open sea often use the stars to plot a course and steer their ships.

SUPER STARGAZING

The way to do this is to find Polaris, which is also called the North Star as it is almost directly above the North Pole. Polaris helps you find north. Of course, if you know which way is north, you can also find east, south and west.

It does take a little bit of time to become skilled at finding stars, so practise every time there is a clear night, and soon you'll be a night-sky navigator.

HOW TO FIND NORTH

1. There are countless stars in the night sky and thousands that we can see. To help identify them, they are put into groups called 'constellations'. The group of stars you need to find in the sky is part of the constellation Ursa Major, and is called the Big Dipper.

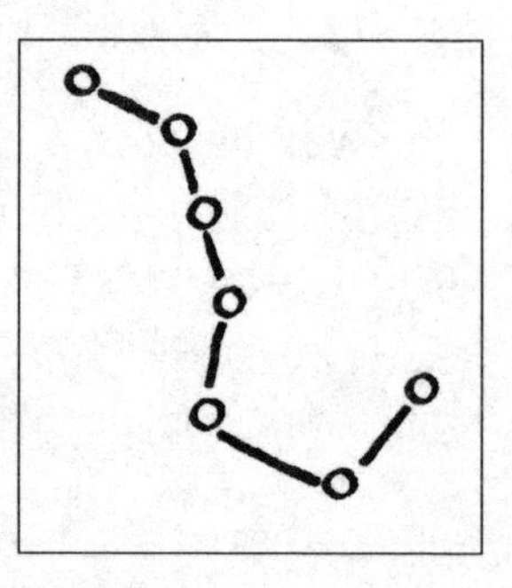

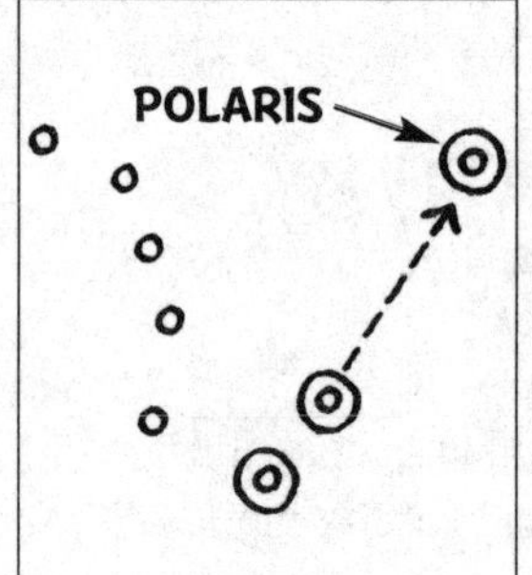

2. Look at the two stars at the right of the Big Dipper. These are called the 'pointer' stars. Now imagine a line drawn between these two stars and continue this line upwards. This line leads you to another, very bright, star. This is Polaris, the North Star.

3. So, to work out which direction north is from where you are standing, turn yourself to face Polaris. You are now facing north.

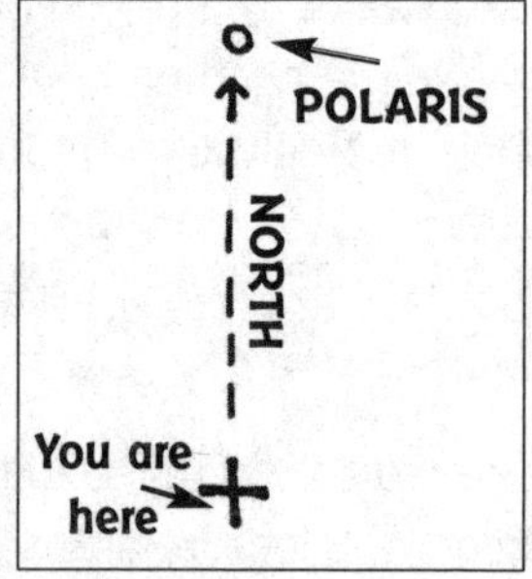

In the southern hemisphere (the part of the Earth that is below the equator), Polaris cannot be seen. Instead, people in the southern hemisphere use a constellation called Crux (also called the Southern Cross) to help them find south.

HOW TO GO THROUGH THE FLOOR

There's no doubt about it, the human mind is an amazing thing. Come to think of it, the human body is pretty incredible, too. However, this simple exercise stops these two, very clever things from working together.

Get together with a friend and try out this cool trick, which will confuse your body and your brain.

WHAT YOU DO

1. Lie on your back on the floor and raise your legs, keeping them straight.

2. Ask your friend to hold your ankles with both hands and lift your legs until they are level with his waist.

3. Shut your eyes and breathe deeply. Ask your friend to hold your legs still in that position for one minute.

4. Tell your friend to lower your legs towards the floor very, very slowly.

Your brain will get impatient, and will send signals telling you that your legs have reached the floor much earlier than they actually have. Then, of course, your legs will keep moving slowly downwards, and you'll be left with the very weird feeling of your legs passing straight through the solid floor.

HOW TO MAKE THE PERFECT PIZZA

Fresh, home-made pizza is truly delicious, and if you think it's difficult to make, think again. Home-made pizza is easy, fun and very tasty. Follow these simple steps and you'll be cooking like a real Italian pizza chef in no time.

Before you start, remember the golden rules of cooking: always get permission from your parents and get an adult's help when dealing with hot ovens and sharp knives.

You Will Need:

• 200 g plain flour • 1 teaspoon dried yeast • a pinch of salt • a pinch of sugar • 1 tablespoon olive oil • 120 ml warm water • olive oil for brushing round the bowl • 2 tablespoons tomato purée • 150 g grated cheese

WHAT YOU DO

1. Pour the flour into a bowl and mix with the yeast. Add the salt and sugar.

2. Make a little dent in the middle and pour in the olive oil and water. Mix together with your hands until you have a lump of dough.

3. Take the dough out of the bowl and put it on a hard surface that you have sprinkled with flour (this will stop the dough sticking). Grab the edge of the dough and fold it over the rest of the dough. Push down into it with the heel of your hand to flatten it. Turn it round a little bit and do this again. This is called 'kneading' the dough, and you should knead for a few minutes.

4. Rub some olive oil around the bowl to stop the dough sticking. Put the dough back in and cover the bowl with a cloth. Leave it for an hour, so the dough has time to rise (this is what happens to dough when you put yeast in it).

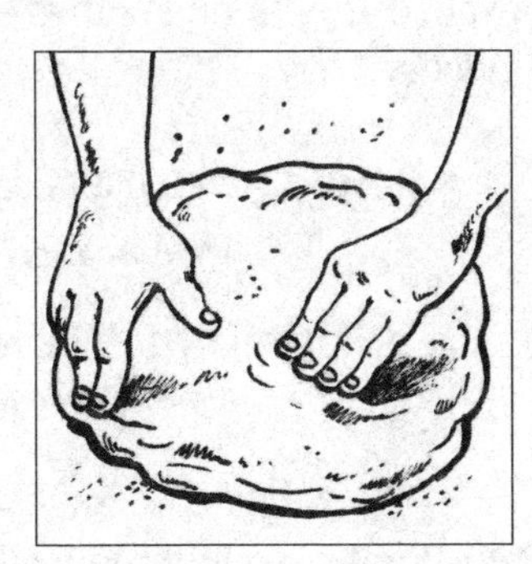

5. Take the dough out and knead it again to get rid of any large air bubbles. Then press and shape the dough with your fingers into a circular pizza shape.

6. Spread the tomato purée over your base and sprinkle the grated cheese over the top of it.

GET 'TOPPING-TASTIC'

Now, the fun really starts – adding the toppings. You can add toppings you are familiar with, such as ham and pineapple, or you can invent completely new pizza flavours. What about a beef and barbecue sauce pizza, or a smoked salmon and cream cheese pizza?

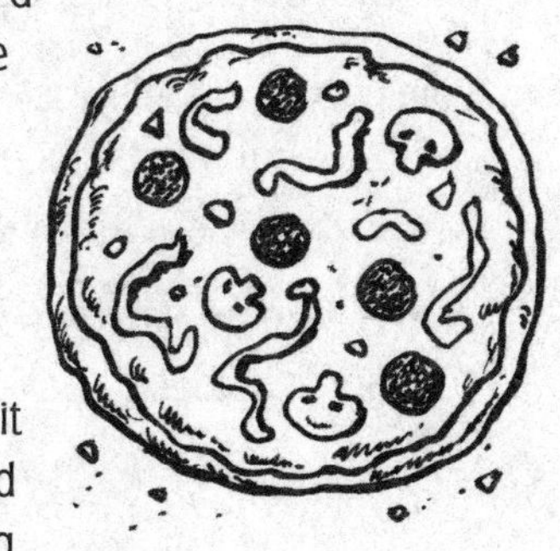

Once the toppings are on, place your pizza on a baking tray in the oven at 220°C (Gas Mark 7) for about 15 minutes. When you take it out, the crust should have browned and the cheese should be bubbling.

HOW TO ESCAPE GETTING INTO TROUBLE FOR NOT DOING YOUR HOMEWORK

If you've not managed to get your homework finished on time, and you are bored of using the same old 'My dog ate it' excuse, try out one of these imaginative new excuses on your teacher:

- 'I was so tired after doing my voluntary work at the old people's home that I fell asleep.'
- 'My mum was looking really tired, so I did all the housework for her.'
- 'I watched a documentary about the destruction of the rainforests, so I decided to help the environment by not using any more paper.'
- 'I was concerned about how hard you work, Sir, and I didn't want to give you any more marking to do.'
- 'My dad thinks I'm clumsy, so he made me play computer games all evening to improve my coordination.'
- 'I was on a special mission for the Government. I can't tell you what it was about, because you don't have security clearance.'

Be warned though, teachers are clever, so don't be surprised if your teacher still doesn't believe your excuse.

HOW TO BUILD A CARD TOWER

This section could be called 'How to Really Annoy Yourself' as there's nothing as stressful as spending a lot of time and effort building up a card tower only to make one wrong move and see it collapse. But when you get it right, it's fantastic and very rewarding. So, try to stay cool as you follow these instructions:

1. Take a set of playing cards. Take out two cards and stand them up, leaning them against each other in an upside-down-V-shape that looks a bit like a tent. They should be about the same width apart at the bottom as your middle three fingers. Try building your card tower on carpet as it gives more friction and the cards will be less likely to fall down.

2. Next, take another two cards and build another tent shape, next to the first. There should be only one finger space between the bottom of each of the two shapes. This is when building the tower can start to get annoying. If the second shape collapses, the chances are it will also knock down your first shape.

3. Once your two tent shapes are standing, lay another card on top of the shapes, resting on the points.

4. The next step is to make another tent shape on top of the other two by using the card you have just laid as the base.

If you have got this far, you are doing very well. You have already made a two-row card tower. One more row and you've done it (unless you want to go even higher).

5. Back at ground level, put another tent shape next to the first two.

6. Lay a card across the top, so that it rests on the points of the second and third tent shapes.

7. Use this as the base to build a second tent shape on the second row.

8. Lay a card across the top of the tent shapes on the second row.

9. Finally, place the last tent shape on top of this card. You now have a three-row tower with three tent shapes on the bottom row, two on the middle row and one on the top row.

HOW TO STYLE OUT A FALL

Have you ever tripped and fallen over in public? If so, you probably found that hearing people laughing at you was more painful than the bruises you collected. Everybody falls down now and then, and it's important to know how to do this without looking silly.

The best way is to make it look as if you fell on purpose. Here are a few ideas of things you can do to avoid the laughter:

- Make your fall look like part of a move by springing straight back up. For example, if you fall on your back, bend your knees, push yourself up and strike a martial arts pose. Then, look at your friends and say, 'I bet you can't do that.'

- If you fall forwards, roll with the fall so that you fall, roll and get up all in one cool move. As soon as you are on your feet, carry on walking as if nothing has happened.

- If you fall flat on your face, shout, 'Come on, everybody, let's see who can do the most press ups!' Then start pushing up and down.

- Wintertime can make things extra hazardous, as the ground can often be slippery with ice or snow. If you fall down in the snow, start moving your arms and legs up and down and pretend that you suddenly decided to make a snow angel.

- To disguise a fall where you end up on your back, stay down, put your hands behind your head and pretend you are having a rest. This can work well in a field, but not so well if you fall down in the middle of a supermarket.

HOW TO PAN FOR GOLD

Imagine the thrill as, through the mud and the dirt of a stream, you catch sight of something bright, yellow and glittering. Gold! The following method for finding gold is called 'panning'. Be warned though, the hunt for gold can be addictive, and people have been known to spend their whole lives searching. If you're going to try your hand at panning for gold, make sure you don't get taken over by this kind of 'gold fever'.

Don't waste time looking for gold where there isn't any – find a stream where gold has been found before. The most famous 'gold rush', where many people found gold nuggets, was in a river in California in the USA. Do some research online to see if there's a good gold-panning spot near where you live.

You Will Need:

- a metal pan (shaped a bit like a soup bowl)
- a small shovel
- a jar with a lid

WHAT YOU DO

1. Find a part of the stream where the water is moving slowly. Panning for gold is about understanding that gold is heavier than the sand, mud and gravel it is found in. The tiny flecks of gold that get swept along by the current sink to the bed of the stream where the water slows down.

2. Using your shovel, dig into the stream bed, lift the dirt out and put it into the pan.

3. Lower your pan into the running water and swirl it around gently. This loosens the sand and stones and the running water carries them away. The gold won't be carried away by the water as its weight makes it sink to the bottom of the pan. You won't get rid of all the sand and pebbles doing this, but you will get rid of most of it.

4. Take the pan out of the water and continue swirling. Tilt the pan slightly so nearly all the water and dirt gradually leave the pan.

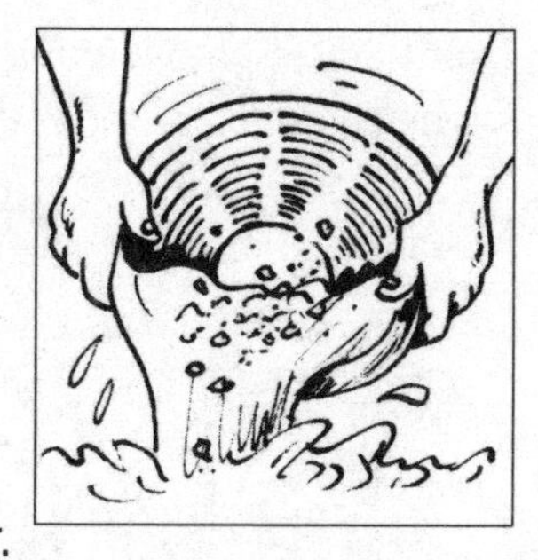

5. Use your fingers to search through the remaining material for tiny pieces of gold. If you find any, carefully remove them and put them in your jar.

HOW TO MAKE A PAPER FIRECRACKER

Origami is the Japanese art of paper folding. Origami artists can make intricate shapes – from beautiful birds, to frogs that really hop – just by folding and creasing paper. This simple origami trick will show you how to create an incredibly loud 'Crack!' sound – like a firework – using just one piece of paper.

You Will Need:

• a piece of A4 paper • scissors • sticky tape

WHAT YOU DO

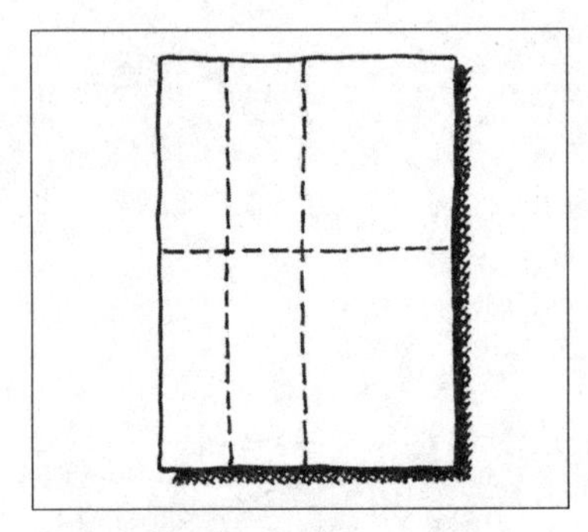

1. Fold the piece of paper in half both ways across the middle, then unfold them again, so there is a cross shape of creases across the middle. Then fold one of the longer sides into the middle and unfold it again.

2. Cut down the two long creases you have made so you have two equally sized strips. These are the bits you need to keep. You could use the other bit of the paper to make another firecracker for a friend.

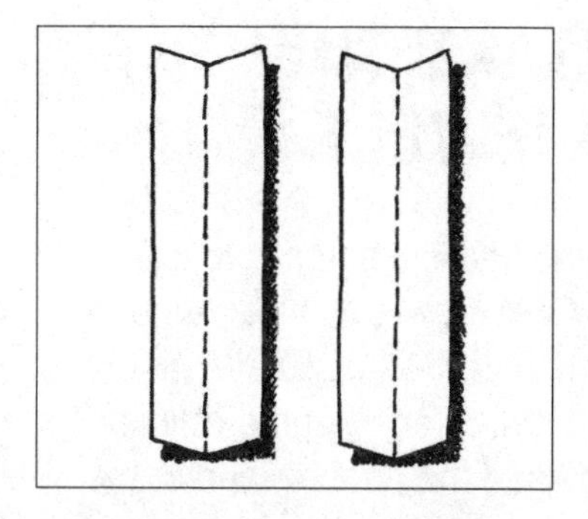

3. Fold each of the two strips in half lengthways. Then unfold them again,

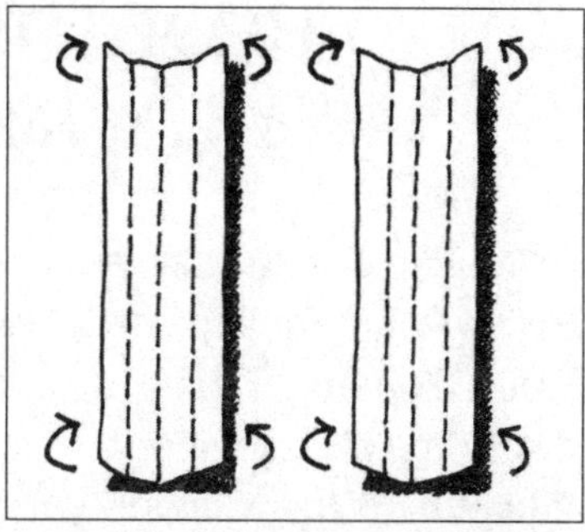

4. Fold each of the long edges into the middle and keep them folded in.

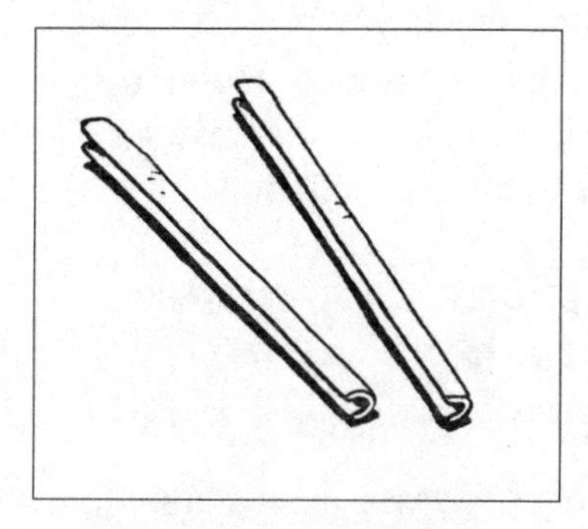

5. Fold each of the strips in half again to form a thick sideways 'V' shape. Your two strips should now look like the picture below.

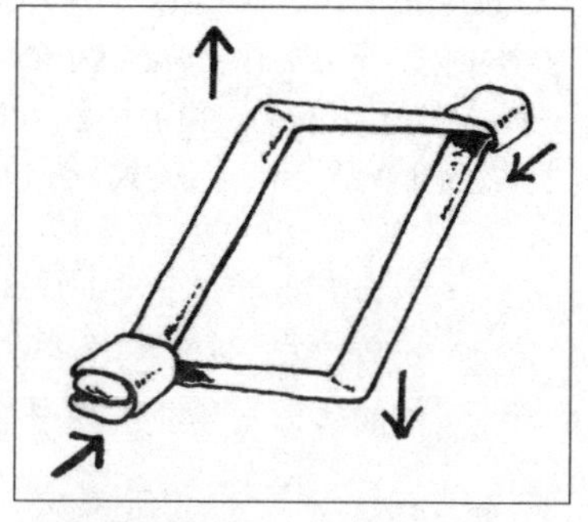

6. Put both strips on top of each other and tape the ends together with sticky tape. Hold both ends tightly and move your hands close together so that the centres of the strips move apart.

7. Pull your hands apart as fast as you can so that the strips smack together. The faster you move your hands, the louder the sound will be. CRACK!

HOW TO TAKE THE CROWN JEWELS

A wonderful collection of priceless treasure belongs to the British Royal Family. The State Crown glistens with nearly 3,000 diamonds. There are rings, bracelets, a sceptre, an orb, the Sword of State and so much more. Together the collection is known as the 'Crown Jewels', and they are housed at the Tower of London.

The most famous attempt to try and steal this precious treasure hoard was carried out by a man named Colonel Blood over 300 years ago. He tried to smuggle the Jewels from the Tower under his cloak, but was caught and imprisoned. Today the Jewels are protected by incredible security. Anyone planning to make off with the Jewels needs to bear in mind that:

- The Tower of London is an ancient, fortified castle, surrounded by two high walls and a moat.
- The Jewels are guarded both by armed guards and the Yeomen Warders, better known as 'Beefeaters', who patrol the Tower dressed in scarlet and black tunics, or scarlet and gold if there's a special occasion.
- There is a control room within the Tower where soldiers constantly watch the Jewels.
- The Jewels are kept in bomb-proof display cases.
- They are protected by high-tech security and you may have to watch out for electronic beams that set off alarms if you cross them and shutters that come crashing down.

As if all this wasn't enough, you'd have to be extra brave to break in at night as, over the centuries, The Tower has been a scene of torture, murder and execution and is said to be the most haunted building in England.

So, how can anyone possibly steal the Crown Jewels when they are so well protected?

Well ...

If ever you go to the Tower, you will see a number of large, black birds. These are the Tower ravens. An ancient legend says that if the ravens ever leave, the Tower will crumble and the Kingdom will fall. So, while everybody is guarding the Crown Jewels, why not steal the ravens and release them far from the Tower? Then, all you have to do is to pick through the rubble of the fallen Tower until you find the Jewels.

Of course, a boy who is the best at everything would never really steal anything, so once you've had your fill of wearing the Jewels and feeling like royalty, make sure you put them back where they belong.

HOW TO BREW YOUR OWN GINGER BEER

When you've been running around in the sunshine, there's no better refreshment than an ice-cold glass of good old-fashioned ginger beer, and it's even better when you've made it yourself. This recipe will make enough ginger beer to fill a large bottle.

You Will Need:

• 450 ml water • 2 heaped tablespoons fresh ginger, peeled and finely chopped • a lemon • 250 g sugar • ½ teaspoon cream of tartar • 800 ml cold water • ½ teaspoon dried yeast

WHAT YOU DO

1. Measure 450 ml of water into a saucepan.

2. Cut the lemon into thick slices and add the slices to the pan with the chopped ginger.

3. Add the sugar and the cream of tartar.

4. Bring your mixture to the boil, stirring it slowly. Then turn the heat down and let it simmer (boil gently) for five minutes. Ask an adult to help you with this bit.

5. Add the 800 ml of cold water and immediately remove the pan from the heat, then sprinkle the yeast over your mixture.

6. Let the pan cool for five minutes, then put a cloth over the top of it and tie it round with string or a large elastic band so it does not touch the water. The mixture now needs to be left for 24 hours. It doesn't need to go in the fridge, but keep it out of direct sunlight.

7. You need a clean plastic bottle for your ginger beer. A 1½ litre plastic cola bottle is fine, but it is very important to clean it thoroughly with hot water. Make sure you use a plastic bottle as glass ones can explode.

8. Strain your mixture through a sieve into a measuring jug and then pour it into the plastic bottle. It is also very important that you leave some empty space at the top of the bottle for the build-up of fizzy gas.

9. Put the lid on your bottle and leave it for two days. About four times each day unscrew the lid a little bit to let the gas out and then screw it on again.

10. Your ginger beer should now be ready to drink. Chill it in the fridge for a while so it's nice and cold before you drink it. Make sure you drink it within three days, while it's still fresh.

HOW TO STAGE A STUNT FIGHT

A stunt fight is a pretend fight. All those punch-ups and martial-arts battles you see in films are not real. They are carefully rehearsed and nobody really gets hit or hurt.

To create your own totally staged stunt fight, find a friend to work with, and follow these tips to get started.

PREPARATION

- The most important thing is safety. Practise all moves slowly and gradually build up your speed. Make sure everyone knows exactly what to do. If there are any falls, practise these slowly so you fall safely, and stick to grass or carpet rather than harder surfaces.

- Keep enough distance between you and your fight partner. There needs to be enough room for each of you to be able to throw a punch or kick without touching each other.

CONVINCE YOUR AUDIENCE

Film stuntmen always know where the camera is. Plan your stunt fight around the audience that's watching to make it look as impressive as possible. Here's how to perform a really convincing pretend punch:

1. Swing your right fist close to the other stunt fighter's face.

2. As you get close to his face with your fist, slap yourself on the chest with your other hand.

3. Do not let your fist come into contact with your partner's face. The slap to your chest will make a loud 'thump', which will make the person watching think it was a real punch.

4. At the same time as the 'thump' sound, your partner should stagger backwards as though he has been hit.

This only works if the people watching are behind you as you throw your pretend punch. If not, they will see you slapping your chest.

STUNT-FIGHT SECRETS

- 'Telegraph' all your moves. 'Telegraphing' means letting your partner know what you are going to do by making a slight movement which he can see but those watching can't. If you are going to pretend to kick him with your left foot, move the foot slightly and look at him to check he has understood. He will be able to know where the next move is coming from.

- 'Synchronize' your moves. This means that you should do things at the same time. If you kick and your friend dives at the same time, in the same direction the kick is going, then it looks as if he has been kicked over. The timing needs to be perfect so – as with everything in stunt fighting – you will need to practise.

HOW TO RECEIVE YOUR KNIGHTHOOD

You kneel on the ground with your head bowed as the person before you clutches a sharp, steel sword. The room is silent as you wait for the weapon to fall.

Sounds terrifying, doesn't it? Believe it or not, this could actually be the greatest moment of your life – the day you receive your knighthood. If it is, then the person raising the sword is none other than the Queen of the United Kingdom herself and, in a few moments, you are about to become a genuine knight.

Knighthoods are awarded for great achievements and have been presented to artists, musicians, actors, sports stars, charity fundraisers and others who have performed their job outstandingly well.

IT'S KNIGHT TIME

The day of your knighthood is called your 'investiture'. It is a very grand, formal occasion and it is important that you know how to behave.

Investitures are usually held at Buckingham Palace in London. Make sure you arrive in plenty of time and that you bring no more than three people to watch you being knighted.

You will be led into the ballroom and will stand with the other people waiting to receive their honour. Once everyone is in place, the Queen will enter the room escorted by two soldiers.

The Yeomen of the Guard, who are the Queen's bodyguards, will also be there.

The national anthem, *God Save the Queen*, is then played, after which a lord calls the name of each person and states the reason they are being knighted.

I DUB THEE ...

When your name is called, step forward and kneel in front of the Queen. She will stand before you, take her sword and place the blade on your right shoulder and then on your left shoulder. This is called 'dubbing' and, as she places the blade on your shoulders, she will say, 'I dub thee Sir (your name).'

Congratulations! You are now a knight. This means you can put 'Sir' in front of your name on letters and emails, and can insist that everyone addresses you as 'Sir', even your parents.

HOW TO MAKE A GIANT CHOC-CHIP COOKIE

If you are a cookie-lover, then you'll know that the best cookies all have two things in common. First, they have lots of chocolate in, and second, they are very, very big.

So, if you plan to make your own cookie, there's only one type to make – a giant choc-chip cookie. Cookie making – even giant cookie making – is quick and easy. Follow these instructions and you'll be munching away in no time.

Warning. When using a hot oven, always use oven gloves and ask an adult to help you.

You Will Need:

• 200 g butter • 135 g caster sugar • 150 g brown sugar • 1 teaspoon vanilla essence • 2 eggs • 250 g plain flour • ½ teaspoon baking powder • ½ teaspoon salt • 150 g chocolate chips • a large cake tin or baking tray with raised sides

WHAT YOU DO

1. Preheat the oven to 180°C / Gas Mark 4. Put the butter, caster sugar, brown sugar and vanilla essence into a bowl. Use a wooden spoon to mix this up as well as you can until it's smooth and creamy.

2. Add the eggs and mix again.

3. Add the flour, baking powder and salt and mix again. Yes, there is an awful lot of mixing to do in this recipe, but the taste of the cookie will make up for tired arms.

4. Next, add your chocolate chips and mix.

5. Grease the bottom of your cake tin or baking tray with butter, and spread the mixture evenly over it to make your giant cookie shape. Don't worry if it's not perfectly round, it will still be delicious.

6. Bake the cookie for 30 minutes, or until golden brown and firm to the touch. All ovens are slightly different so keep an eye on the cookie to make sure it doesn't burn. If you are using a cake tin, your cookie will rise slightly in the oven, so when it is finished it will look like a cross between a cake and a cookie – what a tasty mix!

7. Leave the cookie to cool and then share it with your friends.

HOW TO TIDY YOUR ROOM IN TEN MINUTES FLAT

Follow this ten-minute countdown and you'll have a tidier room in a flash. On your marks, get set, go!

10: Collect everything that's lying around and put it all in one pile on the floor.

09: Go through the pile and put all the rubbish in a bin bag.

08: Scoop up all the dirty clothes and put them in the washing basket. Put any clean clothes in your drawers or wardrobe.

07: If you have comics and bits of paper you want to keep, put them in a neat pile on top of a shelf or cupboard, or in a box.

06: Collect all books, CDs and DVDs and put them on your shelves.

05: Gather up everything that does not belong in your room – dirty cups and plates, brother's toys, and so on – and put them on a tray outside your room to deal with later.

04: Put all your toys and games in a cupboard. If there is not enough room, stack them up neatly against a wall.

03: Straighten the duvet on your bed.

02: Make sure all drawers are closed and do not have bits of clothes sticking out.

01: Have a final look around to make sure you haven't missed anything, then relax. Job done.

HOW TO FIND THE LOCH NESS MONSTER

Loch Ness, home to the legendary Loch Ness Monster, or 'Nessie', is a deep, dark lake in northern Scotland. There have been many reported sightings and even a few photographs of the monster, although no one is sure whether the shapes photographed in the loch are actually of the famous beast or if they are clever fakes. Follow these top tips and maybe you'll be the first to find this mythical monster:

- Find a speedboat and get out onto the water. A boat fitted with sonar equipment is perfect. Sonar allows you to search deep in the water by sending out pulses of sound and recording any objects they bounce off. If Nessie is lurking under the water, sonar will help you find it.

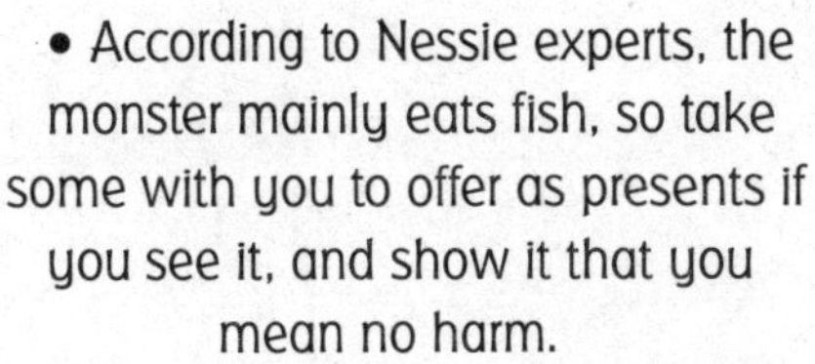

- According to Nessie experts, the monster mainly eats fish, so take some with you to offer as presents if you see it, and show it that you mean no harm.

- Keep your camera with you at all times. If you do spot Nessie, no one will believe you unless you've got photographic evidence.

HOW TO BUST A MOVE ON THE DANCE FLOOR

For a boy who is the best at everything, it's really important to look cool at all times – especially when you're strutting your stuff on the dance floor. Here's a simple hip-hop move that will guarantee that you keep your cool when the music starts.

THE HIP-HOP WAVE

This dance move needs to be done in one fluid motion, so it looks as if a wave is passing through your body. Make sure you put all the following steps together quickly to perform the finished move, otherwise you might look like a robot.

1. Stand with your feet shoulder-width apart and your right arm bent at the elbow. Point the fingers of your right hand down towards the floor.

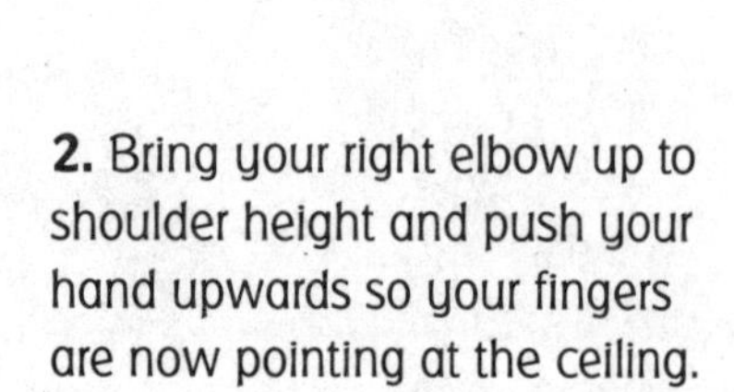

2. Bring your right elbow up to shoulder height and push your hand upwards so your fingers are now pointing at the ceiling.

3. Straighten your right arm so it looks like you are pushing something away from you with the palm of your hand.

4. Raise your right shoulder towards your earlobe and then lower it as you raise your left shoulder. The 'wave' has now passed across your body and you can let your right arm drop down by your side.

5. Lower your left shoulder and lift your left elbow to shoulder height, keep your fingers pointing downwards.

6. Smoothly push your arm out until it is straight.

7. Finally, twist and flick your wrist so that you finish the move with your fingers pointing upwards.

HOW TO BEAT A GORGON

The Gorgons are three mythical creatures named 'Stheno', 'Euryale' and 'Medusa'. These legendary beasts are sisters and all three are incredibly ugly. They have big heads, huge, scary mouths with long tongues hanging out, tusks, and even beards. They also have wings sprouting from their backs, and sharp claws on their hands and feet. Medusa, the most famous of the three, is even worse as her hair is made of live snakes, which hiss and writhe around on her head.

The Gorgons are extremely dangerous creatures to come across, because they have the power to turn anyone who looks at their faces to stone. All around the entrance of the cave where they live there are the frozen, stone bodies of men and animals who have been unfortunate enough to gaze into a Gorgon's face.

Should you be unlucky enough to come across one of these fearsome creatures, you need to know what to do. To defeat a Gorgon, you need a mirror, a hairbrush and some very dark sunglasses. Wearing your sunglasses, carefully approach the Gorgon. Tell her she needs to brush her hair as it's a mess, and then hand her the brush and mirror. When she sees her reflection in the mirror, she will turn herself to stone.

The only problem you will then have is what to do with her next. Stone Gorgons make excellent garden ornaments. When you have defeated her, why not paint your Gorgon in nice bright colours and put her by your front door? If you have a pond, you could stand her next to this with a fishing rod in her hand and tell everyone she's a very ugly garden gnome!

HOW TO PLAY THE 'BILLY GOAT' GAME

This is a quick game that shows you how your senses can become confused when they don't work together. It seems very simple, but is actually quite tricky.

HOW TO PLAY IT

1. Ask your friend to sit with his back to you.

2. Ask him, 'How many horns does the billy goat have?'

3. Press some of the fingers of your right hand into his back.

4. Just by using his sense of touch, and without being able to see your hand, your friend has to guess how many fingers you are holding against his back.

It's surprisingly easy for the brain to make a mistake here, so don't burst out laughing at him if he gets it wrong. Instead, swap places and see for yourself how difficult it can be.

HOW TO MAXIMIZE YOUR POCKET MONEY

However much pocket money your parents give you, one thing is almost certain – it's never enough for all the wonderful things you want to buy. Read on to find out how you can boost the money in your pocket.

The best way to do this is to find something that people will pay you to do. For example, most adults have cars, and it's fairly certain that a lot of these cars will need cleaning. This creates an opportunity for you to earn some money.

PLANNING

- Identify your customers. Parents, relatives and neighbours may all need their cars cleaned. Make sure you ask your parents' permission before you start and always tell them if you are going out to clean someone's car.

- Decide on your price. The best way to get customers is to offer a lower price than your rivals. If your local garage has a car wash, check how much it costs and offer a lower price to your customers.

WASHING THE CAR

You Will Need:

• two buckets • some car shampoo • a sponge • a stiff brush • a 'chamois' leather (pronounced 'shammy') • a lot of water • a hose, if you have one.

Warning. You will get wet while washing cars, so wear some old clothes or overalls to cover your clothes.

WHAT YOU DO

If you do a really good job, people will ask you to clean their cars again. They may even tell other people how good you are. There are six steps to a thorough clean:

1. Fill one bucket with warm water mixed with car shampoo and the other bucket with clean water.

2. Rinse the car with the clean water to remove surface dirt.

3. Dip your brush into the warm, soapy water and give the wheels a good scrub.

4. Clean the rest of the car by dipping the sponge into the soapy water and rubbing the car by moving the sponge in a circular motion. Start at the roof and work downwards.

5. When you have finished, rinse the car with clean water again.

6. Dry the car with the chamois leather.

Top Tip. If you use a hose for rinsing, it will make the job quicker and easier. Make sure all the car doors are shut before you turn the hose on though – you don't want to give the inside of the car a drenching.

HOW TO THROW A CUSTARD PIE

There's nothing to compare with the sheer fun and excitement of a food fight, and there's no food quite so messy as a good, old-fashioned custard pie.

The good news is that custard pies are very easy to make. A secret known to clowns and slapstick comedians is that the custard pies used on TV shows are not actually made out of custard at all. They're great for throwing, but not for eating! Here's how to make your very own pies for throwing.

You Will Need:

- a mixing bowl • shaving foam • yellow food colouring
- paper plates • bin bags or overalls for the pie throwers

WHAT YOU DO

1. Spray some foam into the mixing bowl and mix it with yellow food colouring. This will be your 'custard'. Make sure that all your fellow pie-throwers know that it is not edible.

2. Next, put the yellow foam onto a paper plate and spray a little bit of white foam around the edge for decoration.

3. Shaving foam is quite safe but can sting a little bit. To prevent this, leave your pie to one side for a couple of hours before you throw it to let the sting evaporate.

4. Stage your pie fight outside, on grass, as shaving foam is slippery underfoot. Make sure every pie-thrower covers his clothes with old overalls or a bin bag, as the 'custard' can stain. Don't stand too close to anyone you're aiming at. Balance your pie in the palm of your hand and throw it at your target.

HOW TO BE A BODYGUARD

Being a bodyguard is a job that involves danger and excitement, and requires constant vigilance. If that sounds tempting, and you want to become a bodyguard that no one will mess with, follow these instructions.

1. Look around you constantly. Danger can come from anywhere, at any time.

2. Bodyguards are usually very tall and extremely muscly and strong. Do lots of press-ups and eat lots of protein to make yourself as big and brawny as you can.

3. Always chew gum – bodyguards need to look tough and cool to impress the person they are guarding, and to intimidate everyone else. Wear sunglasses for the same reason, and keep your face set in a mean and moody expression.

4. If you are guarding a celebrity, stop them being mobbed by large groups of their fans. Do this as peacefully as you can.

5. If anything happens, get whoever you are protecting away as quickly as possible. Always plan an escape route, wherever you are.

6. Remember your job is to protect the good guy, not catch the bad guy. If someone attacks and then runs away, don't chase after him, stay with the person you are protecting.

HOW TO DO THE PERFECT PRESS-UP

Press-ups are the perfect exercise, as you don't need any equipment. You can do them anywhere, even if you have only got a couple of minutes to spare, and they are excellent for building your strength.

However, they are only the perfect exercise if you have a perfect technique. It is much better to do a few press-ups and perform them correctly, than to do a lot but carry them out the wrong way.

Here's how to make sure you get maximum benefit from the exercise:

1. Lie face down on the floor.

2. Place your hands underneath your shoulders with the palms touching the floor and fingers facing forwards.

3. Keep your feet together and position them so it is your toes, not the tops of your feet, that are touching the ground.

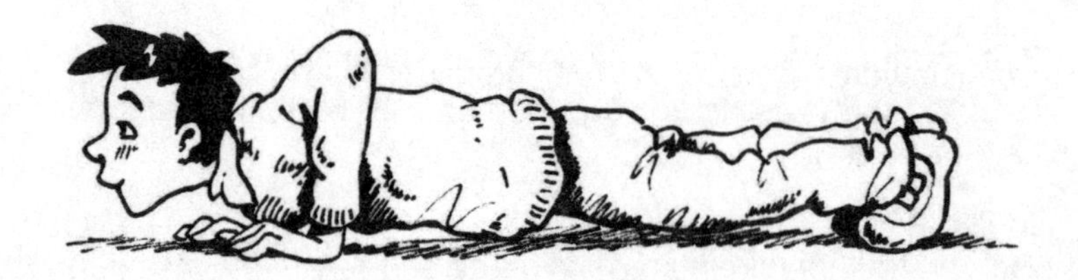

4. Push yourself off the ground by pushing up with your arms until they are straight.

5. Lower yourself slowly by bending your arms at the elbow until your chest hovers just above the floor.

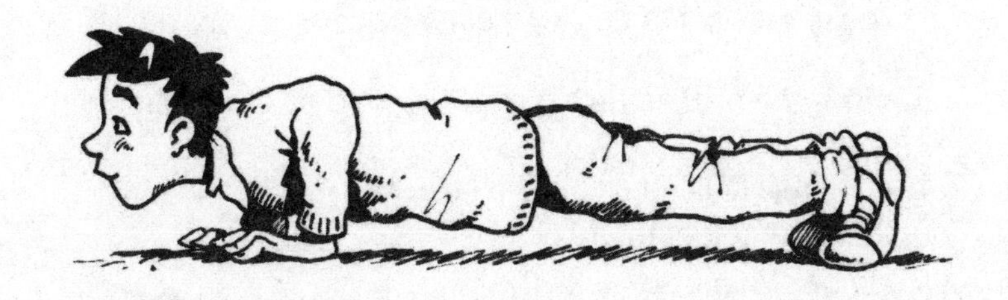

The golden rule of press-ups is to keep your body straight. This takes a bit of practice, and you need to concentrate to make sure you do not stick your bottom up in the air or arch your back upwards. Practise in front of a mirror so you can make sure you are in the correct position.

Top Tip. As with all exercise, it's important not to overdo it. Do not try to break any records at the beginning. Practise your technique by doing a few each day and then build up the number you do slowly.

HOW TO MAKE A SHRUNKEN HEAD

There was a time when certain tribes would attack their enemies, cut off their heads, take the severed heads home as trophies and shrink them. The problem with doing this is that it is dangerous, cruel, very messy and could get you into a lot of trouble. Because of this, here's a shrunken-head method that uses an apple. The result looks just as good and you don't have to go to all the bother of chopping someone's head off.

You Will Need:

• a large apple • 600 ml of water • 60 g salt • 2 tablespoons lemon juice • 30 cm string • wooden or metal skewer • coloured chalk • potato peeler • a small knife

1. Remove the peel of the big apple using a potato peeler.

2. Use a small knife to create the face. Ask an adult to help you. Remember that the head is going to be shrunk, so make the features a bit bigger than you normally would. Make each eye quite deep set as this helps to give the shape of the nose, sticking out from the face. Shape the mouth so the two lips stand out. A nice deep cut between the lips will help them to separate during shrinking.

3. Take a bowl and add the water, salt and lemon juice. Stir until the salt has dissolved, then put the apple in. The head needs to be completely covered by the liquid. If it isn't, add more of the above mixture.

4. To make sure the apple stays completely covered by the liquid at all times, place a plate on top of the bowl.

5. You now need to show a little bit of patience as you have to leave your 'head' in the liquid for a full 24 hours ... the apple head, that is – not your own head!

6. The next bit needs a lot of patience, as the head will take about three weeks to dry. Stick the skewer through the top of the apple, and tie a piece of string to the top of the skewer. Hang it up somewhere it won't be in the way. It needs to be hung up so that the air can get to every side of the apple and stop it from going mouldy.

7. Finally, your shrunken head is ready to decorate. Use coloured chalk to colour in the head and features.

Top Tip. To make your head even more realistic and gruesome, use glue to add some raisins for the eyes and pieces of rice for teeth.

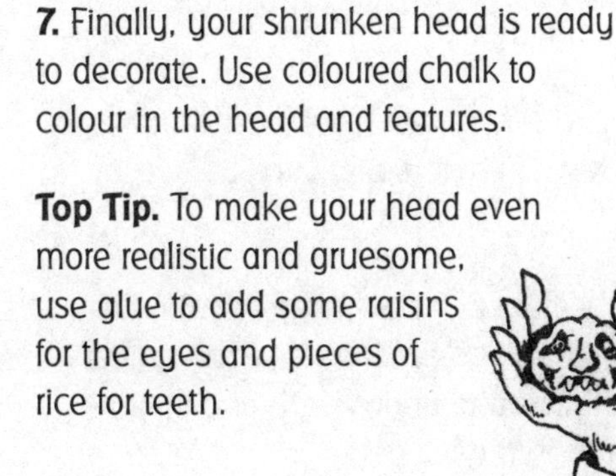

HOW TO PLAY THE TRICK BOX GAME

This creepy game is perfect to play on Halloween, or to spook up a sleepover. The reason it's so terrifying is because the most frightening things are the things you can't see. When you can't see something, the power of the imagination takes over. Here's how to create your trick boxes and give your friends the fright of their lives.

You Will Need:

• 5 cardboard boxes with lids (shoeboxes will work perfectly) • black paper • white paint • a paintbrush • scissors • sticky tape • 5 paper plates • 50 g cold, cooked spaghetti • a small piece of fake fur • a rubber glove • 100 g flour • 10 peeled grapes • one small cauliflower

WHAT YOU DO

1. Cut a hole in the lid of each box, just large enough for someone to put their hand through.

2. Decorate each box by covering it with black paper and painting scary objects on it with white paint, such as bats or skulls.

3. Cut a piece of black paper for each box, large enough to cover the hole, and tape it at one side of the hole. This creates a flap so people can slide their hand underneath and into the holes without seeing what is in the boxes.

4. Put a paper plate in each of the boxes and tape it to the bottom so it doesn't move.

5. Now it's time to add your spooky items. Put the spaghetti on the plate in box one, the fur in box two, the peeled grapes in box three and the cauliflower in box four. Fill the rubber glove up with flour before placing it on the plate in box five.

6. Make sure you create the right atmosphere for the game. Turn the lights down low and play eerie music if you have some. Tell your friends that each box contains a truly gross item that you have taken from a witch's cavern.

7. Each person places their hand into the boxes, one at a time, and tries to guess what the objects are by feeling them. Get ready to hear some screams!

ALSO AVAILABLE ...

The Boys' Book 1:
How To Be The Best
At Everything

ISBN: 978-1-905158-64-5

The Boys' Book 2:
How To Be The Best
At Everything Again

ISBN: 978-1-906082-33-8

The Boys' Book Of Survival:
How To Survive
Anything, Anywhere

ISBN: 978-1-906082-12-3

The Boys' Book Of Spycraft:
How To Be The Best
Secret Agent Ever

ISBN: 978-1-906082-39-0

The Unbeatable Boys' Book:
How To Be The
Ultimate Champion

ISBN: 978-1-906082-69-7